Communicate Abroad

Simon Cookson / Chihiro Tajima

Essential English for Travel and Study

Communicate Abroad—Essential English for Travel and Study

Simon Cookson / Chihiro Tajima

© 2016 Cengage Learning K.K.

ALL RIGHTS RESERVED. No part of this work covered by the copyright herein may be reproduced, transmitted, stored, or used in any form or by any means—graphic, electronic, or mechanical, including but not limited to photocopying, recording, scanning, digitizing, taping, Web distribution, information networks, or information storage and retrieval systems—without the prior written permission of the publisher.

Photo Credits:

p. 17: © Photodisc/Thinkstock; p. 25: © sandr2002/iStock/Thinkstock; p. 41: © Jakub Jirsák/iStock/Thinkstock;
p. 49: © Grotmarsel/iStock/Thinkstock; p. 57: © Pedro antonio Salaverría calahorra/Hemera/Thinkstock;
p. 69: © WestLight/iStock/Thinkstock; p. 85: © moodboard/Thinkstock; p. 93: © Pavel Potapov/Hemera/Thinkstock;
p. 101: © caucasiando/iStock/Thinkstock

For permission to use material from this textbook or product, e-mail to **eltjapan@cengage.com**

ISBN: 978-4-86312-277-2

Cengage Learning K.K.
No. 2 Funato Building 5th Floor
1-11-11 Kudankita, Chiyoda-ku
Tokyo 102-0073
Japan

Tel: 03-3511-4392
Fax: 03-3511-4391

Preface

Welcome to *Communicate Abroad*! Traveling overseas and studying abroad is a lot of fun, and a great way to learn about other countries. This textbook helps you to prepare for travel and study abroad. It has information about other cultures, and many activities to improve your listening, speaking and reading skills.

The main character is a Japanese student, Junko, who goes to study in the US. In each unit, Junko or her friends solve a problem. These are typical problems that Japanese students face when they travel overseas or study abroad. The problems include culture shock, making friends and losing a passport.

Each unit includes important keywords with Japanese translations. You can practice using these keywords in the listening and speaking activities. There is also advice about travel and study abroad. At the end of each unit, there are useful English phrases with Japanese translations, as well as information about using numbers in English.

We hope that you enjoy using this textbook. The aim is to prepare you for travel or study overseas, but this textbook is useful even if you are not going abroad soon. We hope that it helps you to become more independent, more intercultural and a better communicator of English.

『Communicate Abroad』の世界へようこそ！ 海外を旅したり留学に出かけることはとても楽しく、異国について学ぶ素晴らしい方法でもあります。皆さんの海外旅行や留学の準備に役立つように、本書には他の文化に関する情報に加え、リスニング・スピーキング・リーディング能力の向上を目指す数多くのアクティビティーを盛り込んでいます。

メインキャラクターは、アメリカに勉強しに行く日本人学生のジュンコです。各ユニットでは、ジュンコや友人たちが問題を解決します。扱う問題は日本人学生が海外旅行や留学でよく遭遇するもので、例えばカルチャーショックや友人作り、パスポートの紛失などを含んでいます。

各ユニットには重要なキーワードと和訳が含まれていて、リスニングやスピーキングアクティビティーを通して、これらのキーワードを使う練習ができます。海外旅行や留学に関するアドバイスも載せました。各ユニットの最後には、役に立つ英語表現と和訳、また、英語で数字を使う際の情報も加えてあります。

皆さんが楽しみながら本書を使えるようにと願っています。海外旅行や留学の準備を目的としていますが、すぐに海外に行かない人にも役立つテキストです。皆さんがさらに自立し、異文化力を向上させ、より良い英語コミュニケーターになりますように。

Simon Cookson

田島千裕

Contents

Pages		
3		Preface
6		To the Teacher

Pages	Units	Titles
10	Unit 1	My Suitcase Is Overweight
18	Unit 2	I'm Suffering from Jet Lag
26	Unit 3	Each Host Family Is Different
34	Unit 4	I'm Experiencing Culture Shock
42	Unit 5	My Dormitory Is too Noisy
50	Unit 6	How Can I Make Friends?
62	Unit 7	What Should I Talk About?
70	Unit 8	I Feel Homesick
78	Unit 9	How Do I Order Food?
86	Unit 10	I Lost My Passport
94	Unit 11	I Need to Go to Hospital
102	Unit 12	I Don't Want to Leave

58		Review of Units 1–6
110		Review of Units 7–12
114		Preparation for Departure

Topics	Numbers
Airport check-in / Airline baggage rules	Weight
Jet lag / Time zones	Time
Homestays / Host family rules	Telephone
Cultural differences / Stages of culture shock	Dates
Dormitory life / Suggestions and requests	Size
Making friends / Activities overseas	Volume
Talking with people / Conversation topics	1–10,000
Missing Japan / Dealing with homesickness	10,000+
Ordering and paying in a restaurant	Money
Losing something / Valuable possessions	Distance
Going to a clinic or hospital / Health advice	Temperature
Preparing to return to Japan / Benefits of going abroad	Decimals & Fractions

To the Teacher

Communicate Abroad is aimed at high-beginner or low-intermediate level students, and helps prepare them for travel or study abroad. This textbook covers a range of situations, starting with flying to another country, then living abroad, and finally leaving the host country. Those students who are not going abroad can still benefit from this textbook, as it provides English language and practice opportunities in a variety of contexts.

In each unit of the textbook, Junko—the main character—and her international friends solve a problem. The aim of the textbook is to provide students with the language and skills they need to overcome problems during their own travel/study aboard. It therefore helps students to become more independent and more confident in navigating life overseas. Also, this textbook gives them a realistic idea of some of the issues involved in travel/study abroad.

There are 12 units in the textbook, and each unit has eight pages. For a 15-lesson course, it may not be possible to cover all the material in class, so teachers may want to assign the Useful Expressions pages at the end of the unit as self-study or homework. For a 30-lesson course, we recommend spending two lessons on each unit. In this case, the Useful Expressions pages may be covered in class. If more material is needed, the Teacher's Manual contains the Vocabulary Review activities for each unit. The Teacher's Manual also includes two 50-item tests.

Unit Overview

Each unit has the same format:

▶ Warm-up

This section has three questions that introduce the topic of the unit. For lower-level classes, teachers can provide model answers to the students, and students can write down their answers before speaking.

▶ Vocabulary

The Vocabulary introduces 10 keywords related to the topic of the unit.

Keywords

The Keywords section includes short Japanese definitions so that students can understand each word quickly.

Pronunciation

The Pronunciation section allows students to practice saying the words correctly.

Definitions

In the Definitions section, students match the keywords to English definitions. This activity lets students use the keywords in an English context, and helps them to consolidate the words.

Extra

The Extra section introduces more information for students who finish the Definitions task early, or who wish to expand their knowledge of the vocabulary items they are learning.

► Dialog

The Dialog has a short conversation between two characters that allows students to practice listening and speaking skills.

Listening

Students listen to the dialog and answer three questions. For lower-level classes, teachers may want to play the audio twice.

Speaking

The dialog contains simple but natural language. The substitution items in the table allow students to practice the dialog several times. Many of the substitution items are commonly used expressions. This activity helps students to improve their fluency and build automacity.

Discussion

There are three questions. The first question usually refers back to the dialog. The second question personalizes one of the ideas from the dialog. The third question is usually a link to the Passage, which is on the next two pages. If the Discussion activity is difficult for students, the teacher can provide model answers to show students what kind of responses are appropriate. Note that answers will vary for some questions, especially those that ask about personal experiences. For higher-level classes, teachers can encourage students to ask extra follow-up questions such as:

- "Have you ever had an experience like this?"
- "When/Where did it happen?"
- "What happened?"
- "Tell me about it."
- "What did you do?"

▶ Passage

The Passage contains important information related to the topic of the unit. The information is presented as a gap-fill speaking activity that students do in pairs.

Pairwork

The Pairwork activity contains some of the keywords in natural sentences, and allows students to practice pronunciation by reading aloud. It is important that students do this activity as a speaking/listening exercise, and do not look at their partner's text until they have finished. For the first unit, we recommend setting this activity up carefully. After two or three units, students should be able to do the activity smoothly.

Checking

In the Checking section, the teacher can use the audio to check the answers and the pronunciation of any difficult words.

Comprehension

The Comprehension section contains questions that are designed to check students' understanding of the content of the Passage. If there is time, this can be done in class. Alternatively, teachers may want to set it for homework.

▶ Message & Advice from Junko

These speech bubbles include comments and advice that are useful for students overseas. The comments and advice link back to the problem situation in the Dialog. Junko is a positive character, who solves problems and learns from her mistakes. Therefore, these comments make each unit end in a positive way. It is important for students to feel that problems can be solved, and this section gives students hints about how to deal with or prevent problems. Teachers may want to spend time talking with students about the ideas in this section as they contain important messages.

▶ Useful Expressions

These two pages provide extra vocabulary and expressions related to the topic of the unit.

Phrases on the Topic

This section has many questions and sentences with Japanese translations. Some of the expressions are presented as a question and response. Using the audio, students can listen to the expressions and repeat them, which helps improve their pronunciation and fluency. If there is time, this section can be done in class. Alternatively, teachers may want to set it for homework. For more advanced students, teachers can point out that other words can be substituted into many of the phrases. In Unit 1, for example, "Where is the check-in counter?" can be used to practice a variety of expressions, such as: "Where is gate 35?" "Where is the elevator?" and "Where is the bathroom?"

Numbers

This section presents useful language related to numbers. Being able to use numbers is an important skill for travel overseas, so each unit looks at different types of numbers, such as weight, time, telephone numbers, and so on. Depending on the needs of the students, teachers may want to omit some of these sections. For example, students going to Australia do not need to learn about temperatures in Fahrenheit. If there is time, this section can be done in class. Alternatively, teachers may want to set it for homework.

Review Units

There are two review units (one after Units 1–6 and the other after Units 7–12) so that students can practice some of the keywords, phrases and numbers again.

Preparation for Departure

At the end of the textbook, there is a checklist of things that students should do before going abroad. This section also includes questions about the students' goals for travel/study abroad, their worries and things they are looking forward to. Teachers may want to use this section as part of a pre-departure orientation.

Downloadable Audio Files

Please explain the following instructions to your students.

For activities with a headset icon (00), audio files are available at

http://cengage.jp/elt/ListeningSpeaking/

You can download audio files (MP3) to your computer as outlined below.
1. Visit the website above.
2. Click the cover image or the book title (Communicate Abroad).
3. Click "Audio MP3 (音声ファイル)."
4. Click the link to the file you would like to download.

Use the QR code to directly access audio files.

Unit 1
My Suitcase Is Overweight

This unit is about a problem at the airport check-in. There is also information about airline baggage rules.

Warm-up ▶ Ask these questions to a partner.

1. Do you have a suitcase? If so, what does it look like?
2. If you stay abroad for a month, what might you take in your suitcase?
3. What is the airline weight limit for one suitcase?

Vocabulary

Keywords Do you know the meanings of the words below? Check (✓) any ones that are difficult for you to understand.

1. ☐ baggage [n] ▶ 手荷物
2. ☐ boarding pass [n] ▶ 搭乗券
3. ☐ carry-on bag [n] ▶ 機内に持ち込む鞄
4. ☐ checked baggage [n] ▶ 預ける手荷物
5. ☐ check-in [n] ▶ 搭乗手続き、チェックイン
6. ☐ excess baggage [n] ▶ 超過手荷物
7. ☐ overweight [adj] ▶ 重量超過の
8. ☐ passenger [n] ▶ 乗客
9. ☐ prohibited [adj] ▶ 禁止された
10. ☐ rule [n] ▶ 規則

Pronunciation Listen and repeat the words above. Say each one clearly.

Definitions — Match each word in the box to the best definition below. The first one has been done for you.

| baggage | boarding pass | ~~carry-on bag~~ | checked baggage | check-in |
| excess baggage | overweight | passenger | prohibited | rule |

1. _carry-on bag_ — a bag that a passenger can carry onto the airplane
2. _____ — too heavy
3. _____ — a person who buys a ticket to fly on an airplane
4. _____ — suitcases and bags, also called "luggage"
5. _____ — a card that a passenger needs to get on an airplane
6. _____ — something that tells you what you are allowed to do
7. _____ — suitcases and bags that are heavier or larger than airline limits
8. _____ — giving your suitcases to airport staff and getting a boarding pass
9. _____ — not allowed or permitted
10. _____ — suitcases and bags carried in the baggage section of an airplane

Extra: The prefix "over-" at the start of a word means "too much of something." For example: "overweight" (adj) means "too heavy"; "oversleep" (v) means "to sleep too long"; and "overeat" (v) means "to eat too much."

Dialog

Listening — Junko is taking an international flight, and is at the airport check-in counter. Listen to the dialog, then answer the questions below.

 03

1. Where is Junko flying to?
   _____

2. How many pieces of baggage does Junko have?
   _____

3. What is the problem?
   _____

Speaking Listen to the dialog again and read along. Then, read it aloud with a partner several times. Each time you read, change the underlined words (1–4) using the table below.

Check-in agent:	¹Good morning. Where are you flying today?
Junko:	Hi. I'm going to ²Los Angeles.
Check-in agent:	Can I see your ticket and passport, please?
Junko:	Sure. Here you are.
Check-in agent:	Thank you. How many pieces of baggage do you have?
Junko:	I have ³one suitcase and one carry-on bag.
Check-in agent:	OK. Can you put the suitcase here, please?
Junko:	Sure.
Check-in agent:	Your suitcase is overweight. I have to ask you to pay for the excess baggage.
Junko:	Oh, really? How much do I have to pay?
Check-in agent:	It's ⁴50 dollars, madam.
Junko:	OK. Here you go.
Check-in agent:	Thank you. This is your boarding pass. Enjoy your flight!
Junko:	Thanks.

1	2	3	4
Good afternoon.	Vancouver	a suitcase and a handbag	115 dollars
Good evening.	Tokyo	just one suitcase	75 pounds
Hello.	London	a suitcase and this shopping bag	60 euros

Discussion Think about the dialog above, then discuss these questions with a partner.

1. In the dialog, why did Junko pay extra money?
2. Have you ever had an experience like this?
3. Do you know any other rules about airline baggage?

Passage

Pairwork Student A and Student B have the same passage, but the gaps are different. Take turns reading the sentences aloud to your partner, and write the missing words in the gaps.

Student A

Airline Baggage Rules

Airlines have rules for the size and weight of baggage. There are also rules for how 1._____ pieces of baggage passengers can take. For carry-on bags, many airlines let you take one handbag or shopping bag, and 2._____ other bag. Usually, a carry-on bag should weigh no more than 10 kilograms.

The rules for checked baggage depend on the class of your 3._____. In economy class, each passenger can usually take one or two pieces of checked baggage, with a maximum weight of 23 4._____ per bag or suitcase. First class and business class passengers can take more baggage.

When you pack your carry-on bags, remember that many things are 5._____. For example, you must not carry knives or scissors in your carry-on bags. There are rules about liquids, too. You 6._____ check the airline website for information about prohibited items.

Different airlines have different baggage rules. Also, you can usually take more baggage on 7._____ flights than domestic flights. If your baggage is overweight, or your bags are too big, you must pay an excess baggage charge. This can be 8._____, so check the rules with your airline before you fly!

Pairwork Student A and Student B have the same passage, but the gaps are different. Take turns reading the sentences aloud to your partner, and write the missing words in the gaps.

Student B

Airline Baggage Rules

Airlines have rules for the [1]_____ and weight of baggage. There are also rules for how many pieces of baggage passengers can take. For carry-on [2]_____, many airlines let you take one handbag or shopping bag, and one other bag. Usually, a carry-on bag should weigh no more than [3]_____ kilograms.

The rules for checked baggage depend on the class of your ticket. In economy class, each passenger can usually take one or two pieces of [4]_____ baggage, with a maximum weight of 23 kilograms per bag or suitcase. First class and business class passengers can take more [5]_____.

When you pack your carry-on bags, remember that many things are prohibited. For example, you must not carry knives or scissors in your [6]_____ bags. There are rules about liquids, too. You should check the airline website for information about prohibited items.

Different [7]_____ have different baggage rules. Also, you can usually take more baggage on international flights than domestic flights. If your baggage is [8]_____, or your bags are too big, you must pay an excess baggage charge. This can be expensive, so check the rules with your airline before you fly!

My Suitcase Is Overweight | Unit 1

Checking — Listen to the passage on the previous pages and check your answers.

Comprehension — Think about the passage, then answer the questions below.

1. How many carry-on bags can each passenger have?
   _____

2. What is the maximum weight of the carry-on bag?
   _____

3. How many pieces of checked baggage can each economy class passenger have?
   _____

4. What is the maximum weight of each checked bag or suitcase for economy class?
   _____

5. What must you not put in carry-on bags?
   _____

6. What should you do before your trip?
   _____

Message from Junko

I put a hair dryer and lots of shampoo in my suitcase, so it was really heavy. Actually, I didn't need to take so many things.

Advice from Junko

Check the airline homepage for information about airline baggage rules, and weigh your bags before you leave home!

Useful Expressions

Phrases on the Topic — Below are some useful phrases related to this unit. Check (✓) any ones that are difficult for you to understand.

Airport Check-in

1. ☐ Where is the check-in counter? — チェックインカウンターはどこですか。
2. ☐ Where are you flying? — 渡航先はどこですか。
   ☐ — I'm going to Vancouver. — バンクーバーに行きます。
3. ☐ Here is your boarding pass. — これがあなたの搭乗券です。
4. ☐ Do you have any aisle seats? — 通路側の空席はありますか。
5. ☐ What time does boarding start? — 搭乗開始は何時ですか。
   ☐ — Boarding starts at 12:45 at gate 35. — 搭乗は12時45分に35番ゲートで開始します。
6. ☐ Please take the shuttle bus to the other terminal. — もう1つのターミナルまではシャトルバスをご利用ください。

Baggage

7. ☐ How many bags do you want to check in? — 預けたい鞄はいくつですか。
   ☐ — I have two suitcases. — スーツケースが2つです。
8. ☐ I have one carry-on bag. — 機内に持ち込む鞄が1つあります。
9. ☐ What's the weight of your suitcase? — あなたのスーツケースの重さはどれくらいですか。
   ☐ — It's 22 kilograms. — 22キロです。
10. ☐ How heavy is the carry-on bag? — 機内に持ち込む鞄の重さはどれくらいですか。
    ☐ — It's 15 pounds. — 15ポンドです。
11. ☐ Your suitcase is overweight. — あなたのスーツケースは重量超過しています。
12. ☐ Your carry-on bag is too large. — 機内に持ち込むあなたの鞄は大きすぎます。
13. ☐ You must pay an excess baggage charge. — 超過手荷物料金を支払わなければなりません。

Rules

14. ☐ Knives and scissors are prohibited. — ナイフとハサミは禁止されています。
15. ☐ Smoking is prohibited. — 喫煙は禁止されています。

Pronunciation — Listen and repeat the phrases above. Say each one clearly.

16

Numbers — Weight

Below are two systems for measuring weight: the metric and customary systems. Japan uses the metric system, but the US uses the customary system.

Metric System

gram (g)
kilogram (kg) → 1 kg = 1,000 g

Useful Conversions

1 kg = 35.3 oz
1 kg = 2.2 lb

Customary System

ounce (oz)
pound (lb) → 1 lb = 16 oz

Useful Conversions

1 oz = 28.4 g
1 lb = 454 g

Notes

- The spelling of some words is different in different countries. For example, the spelling is "kilogram" in the US and "kilogramme" in the UK.
- In the UK, there is another unit for measuring people's weight: "stone." 1 stone equals 14 pounds. So 10 stone equals 140 pounds or about 64 kilograms.
- In the UK, the customary system is called the "imperial system."

Pronunciation

Listen and repeat the following weights. Say each one clearly.

1. 5 kg
2. 100 g
3. 8 oz
4. about 50 lb
5. 23 kg
6. 51 lb
7. 10 kg
8. 22 lb
9. about 500 g
10. 17.7 oz

Unit 2
I'm Suffering from Jet Lag

This unit is about jet lag.
There is also information about time zones
and time differences between cities
around the world.

Warm-up ▶ Ask these questions to a partner.

1. Have you ever been on a long flight? If so, how long was the flight?
2. If you have a long flight, how might you feel?
3. Which countries do you want to visit? Why?

Vocabulary

Keywords Do you know the meanings of the words below? Check (✓) any ones that are difficult for you to understand.

1. ☐ caffeine [n]   ▶ カフェイン
2. ☐ fatigued [adj]   ▶ 疲労している
3. ☐ have a headache [v+n] ▶ 頭痛がする
4. ☐ have a stomachache [v+n] ▶ 腹痛がする
5. ☐ irritable [adj]   ▶ 怒りっぽい
6. ☐ jet lag [n]   ▶ 時差ボケ
7. ☐ prevent [v]   ▶ 妨げる
8. ☐ suffer from [v]   ▶ (痛みなど) に苦しむ
9. ☐ symptom [n]   ▶ 症状
10. ☐ time zone [n]   ▶ 標準時間帯、タイムゾーン

Pronunciation Listen and repeat the words above. Say each one clearly.

Unit 2 — I'm Suffering from Jet Lag

Definitions

Match each word in the box to the best definition below. The first one has been done for you.

| caffeine | fatigued | have a headache | have a stomachache | irritable |
| jet lag | prevent | suffer from | symptom | time zone |

1. ___jet lag___ — feeling tired after a long flight across time zones
2. _____ — to have a pain in the stomach
3. _____ — feeling very tired
4. _____ — an area of the world where the time is the same
5. _____ — to have a pain in the head
6. _____ — becoming angry or troubled easily
7. _____ — something in tea and coffee which makes people more active
8. _____ — to feel bad because of a pain or sickness
9. _____ — a feeling or a change in your body that shows you are sick
10. _____ — to stop something from happening

Extra: Use the verb "have" with nouns such as "headache," but use the verb "feel" with adjectives such as "irritable." For example: "I have a headache and I feel irritable."

Dialog

Listening: Junko has just arrived in the US, and is talking with another international student, Carlos. Listen to the dialog, then answer the questions below.

1. Did Junko enjoy dinner last night?
   _____

2. Did Junko sleep well?
   _____

3. What is Junko suffering from?
   _____

19

Speaking

Listen to the dialog again and read along. Then, read it aloud with a partner several times. Each time you read, change the underlined words (1–4) using the table below.

Carlos: Hi Junko. ¹What's the matter?

Junko: Yesterday, my host family made a nice dinner to welcome me but I wasn't hungry.

Carlos: Oh, that doesn't sound good.

Junko: Then last night, I didn't sleep well. I woke up at ² 3 a.m. and couldn't get back to sleep.

Carlos: ³That's a shame. I think you're suffering from jet lag.

Junko: Jet lag? What's that?

Carlos: Jet lag makes you tired when you fly to a different time zone. Sometimes it's difficult to sleep for a few days.

Junko: Really? What should I do?

Carlos: Well I think you should tell your host family how you feel.

Junko: OK, Carlos. But right now, I ⁴have a headache!

1	2	3	4
What's the problem?	3:15	That's too bad.	feel sleepy
What's up?	4 o'clock	I'm sorry about that.	have a stomachache
What happened?	4:30	I'm sorry to hear that.	feel irritable

Discussion Think about the dialog above, then discuss these questions with a partner.

1. In the dialog, why was Junko not feeling well?
2. When do people suffer from jet lag?
3. Have you ever experienced jet lag?

I'm Suffering from Jet Lag | Unit 2

Passage

 Pairwork — Student A and Student B have the same passage, but the gaps are different. Take turns reading the sentences aloud to your partner, and write the missing words in the gaps.

Student A

Time Zones & Jet Lag

The world is divided into 24 one-hour time zones. All the places in one time zone have the same ¹._____. Japan is in one time zone, but some large countries are in several time zones.

There is a time difference between cities in different ²._____. If the time is 8 p.m. in Tokyo, it is 1 a.m. in Honolulu. So the time difference between Tokyo and Honolulu is 19 ³._____.

If you fly across many time zones, jet lag makes you tired. This happens if you fly east to west, or ⁴._____ to east. However, it is not a problem if you fly north to south.

Jet lag usually lasts two or three ⁵._____, but may continue for a week. There are many symptoms. It is difficult to sleep at night, but you feel sleepy in daytime. You ⁶._____ troubled, irritable or fatigued. You are not hungry, and you might have a headache.

How can you prevent ⁷._____? In the airplane, wear loose clothes, drink water or fruit juice, and walk around when possible. Do not drink alcohol or caffeine. After the ⁸._____, focus on local time and go outside in sunlight.

Pairwork Student A and Student B have the same passage, but the gaps are different. Take turns reading the sentences aloud to your partner, and write the missing words in the gaps.

Student B

Time Zones & Jet Lag

The world is divided into [1.] _____ one-hour time zones. All the places in one time zone have the same time. Japan is in one time zone, but some large countries are in several [2.] _____ .

There is a time difference between cities in different countries. If the time is 8 p.m. in Tokyo, it is 1 a.m. in Honolulu. [3.] _____ the time difference between Tokyo and Honolulu is 19 hours.

If you fly across many time zones, jet lag makes you [4.] _____ . This happens if you fly east to west, or west to east. However, it is not a problem if you fly north to [5.] _____ .

Jet lag usually lasts two or three days, but may continue for a week. There are many [6.] _____ . It is difficult to sleep at night, but you feel sleepy in daytime. You feel troubled, irritable or fatigued. You are not hungry, and you might have a [7.] _____ .

How can you prevent jet lag? In the airplane, wear loose clothes, drink water or fruit juice, and [8.] _____ around when possible. Do not drink alcohol or caffeine. After the flight, focus on local time and go outside in sunlight.

I'm Suffering from Jet Lag | Unit 2

Checking   Listen to the passage on the previous pages and check your answers.

Comprehension   Think about the passage, then answer the questions below.

1. How many time zones are there in the world?
   _____

2. If it is 3 a.m. in Honolulu, what time is it in Tokyo?
   _____

3. Is jet lag a problem on an 11-hour flight from Tokyo to Los Angeles? Why or why not?
   _____

4. Is jet lag a problem on a 10-hour flight from Tokyo to Sydney? Why or why not?
   _____

5. What are three symptoms of jet lag?
   _____

6. What are three things you can do to prevent jet lag?
   _____

Message from Junko
When I flew to America, I suffered from jet lag. I changed my watch to the local time, and went outside every day for a walk. After a few days, I felt fine.

Advice from Junko
Try to prevent jet lag, so that you can start your time abroad smoothly!

Useful Expressions

Phrases on the Topic — Below are some useful phrases related to this unit. Check (✓) any ones that are difficult for you to understand.

Time

1. ☐ What's the local time? — 現地は何時ですか。

2. ☐ What's the time difference? — 時差は何時間ですか。
   ☐ — Japan is five hours ahead of here. — 日本はここよりも5時間進んでいます。
   ☐ — Japan is six hours behind here. — 日本はここよりも6時間遅れています。

3. ☐ I'm suffering from jet lag. — 私は時差ボケしています。

Sleep

4. ☐ How did you sleep? — よく眠れましたか。
   ☐ — I slept well. — よく眠れました。
   ☐ — I couldn't get to sleep. — なかなか寝つけませんでした。
   ☐ — I couldn't sleep at all. — 一睡もできませんでした。
   ☐ — I kept waking up. — 何度も起きてしまいました。
   ☐ — I woke up in the middle of the night. — 夜中に目が覚めました。

5. ☐ I should go to bed soon. — 私はもうすぐ寝るべきです。

Sickness

6. ☐ How do you feel? — 気分はどうですか。
   ☐ — I feel tired. — 疲れています。
   ☐ — I feel sick. — 体調が悪いです。
   ☐ — I feel depressed. — 憂鬱な気分です。
   ☐ — I have no energy. — やる気が起きません。

7. ☐ What are your symptoms? — どんな症状がありますか。
   ☐ — I have a sore throat. — 喉が痛いです。
   ☐ — I have no appetite. — 食欲がありません。

Pronunciation — Listen and repeat the phrases above. Say each one clearly.

Unit 2 — I'm Suffering from Jet Lag

Numbers | Time

Below are two ways of telling the time: the 12-hour and 24-hour clocks. The US uses the 12-hour clock, but many countries use the 24-hour clock, especially at stations and airports.

12-Hour Clock

1 a.m.	=	one a.m.
2:15 a.m.	=	two-fifteen a.m.
6 a.m.	=	six a.m.
12 p.m.	=	noon / twelve p.m.
3:30 p.m.	=	three-thirty p.m.
4:45 p.m.	=	four-forty-five p.m.
9 p.m.	=	nine p.m.
11:50 p.m.	=	eleven-fifty p.m.
12 a.m.	=	midnight / twelve a.m.

24-Hour Clock

01:00	=	zero-one-hundred
02:15	=	zero-two-fifteen
06:00	=	zero-six-hundred
12:00	=	twelve-hundred
15:30	=	fifteen-thirty
16:45	=	sixteen-forty-five
21:00	=	twenty-one-hundred
23:50	=	twenty-three-fifty
24:00	=	twenty-four-hundred

Notes

- For 1:00 you can also say "one o'clock," but for 1:20 you cannot say "one twenty o'clock."
- For 2:15 you can also say "a quarter after two" in the US, and "a quarter past two" in the UK.
- For 3:30 you can also say "half past three."
- For 4:45 you can also say "a quarter to five."
- For 11:50 you can also say "ten to twelve."

Pronunciation

Listen and repeat the following times. Say each one clearly.

1. 4:25 a.m.
2. 08:45
3. 11 a.m.
4. 10:30
5. about 6 p.m.
6. 17:15
7. 8:30 p.m.
8. 22:00
9. 10:45 a.m.
10. 5:15 p.m.

Unit 3
Each Host Family Is Different

This unit is about homestays. There is also information about typical host family rules.

Warm-up ▶ Ask these questions to a partner.

1. Have you ever done a homestay before?
2. What are good points about staying with a host family?
3. What difficulties might you have in a homestay?

Vocabulary

Keywords Do you know the meanings of the words below? Check (✓) any ones that are difficult for you to understand.

1. ☐ be responsible for [v+adj] ▶ (物事) に責任を持つ
2. ☐ chore [n] ▶ 家事
3. ☐ clear the table [v+n] ▶ 食卓を片付ける
4. ☐ dislike [n] ▶ 嫌いなもの
5. ☐ do the laundry [v+n] ▶ 洗濯をする
6. ☐ have an allergy [v+n] ▶ アレルギーがある
7. ☐ homestay [n] ▶ ホームステイ
8. ☐ host family [n] ▶ ホストファミリー
9. ☐ in advance [adv] ▶ 事前に
10. ☐ set the table [v+n] ▶ 食卓を整える

Pronunciation Listen and repeat the words above. Say each one clearly.

Each Host Family Is Different Unit 3

Definitions Match each word in the box to the best definition below. The first one has been done for you.

| be responsible for | chore | clear the table | dislike | do the laundry |
| have an allergy | ~~homestay~~ | host family | in advance | set the table |

1. _homestay_ — living in the house of a local family during your stay abroad
2. _____ — something which you do not like
3. _____ — to put knives, forks and plates on the table before a meal
4. _____ — a family that you stay with during your time abroad
5. _____ — housework, such as cleaning your bedroom or washing your clothes
6. _____ — to wash clothes, sheets and so on
7. _____ — to have a strong reaction to a food or plant
8. _____ — before a set time
9. _____ — to take knives, forks and plates off the table after a meal
10. _____ — to have something you must do such as a task or job

Extra Some English words, such as "dislike," can be a noun or verb. Noun example: "What are your likes and dislikes?" Verb example: "I like tea but I dislike coffee."

Dialog

Listening Junko is in her host family's house, and is talking with her host mother, Penny. Listen to the dialog, then answer the questions below.

13

1. Which meal are Junko and Penny going to eat?
   _____

2. Is there a communication problem?
   _____

3. What does Junko have to do?
   _____

| Speaking | Listen to the dialog again and read along. Then, read it aloud with a partner several times. Each time you read, change the underlined words (1–4) using the table below. |

Penny: Junko, dinner will be ready soon.
Junko: What are we having?
Penny: This evening we're having ¹lasagna and salad.
Junko: Great. ²Can I help?
Penny: Can you please set the table?
Junko: Sit the table? I'm sorry, I don't understand. ³Could you say that again?
Penny: Oh, sure. Can you set the table? Please put the knives, forks and plates on the table.
Junko: Ah, now I understand. Where are they?
Penny: The knives and forks are ⁴here. The plates are on the shelf.
Junko: Sure, I'll do it now.
Penny: Thanks.

1	2	3	4
spaghetti with meatballs	How can I help?	Could you repeat that?	over there
meatloaf	What can I do?	Please repeat that.	in the drawer
chicken and mashed potatoes	Let me help.	Once more, please.	on the counter

| Discussion | Think about the dialog above, then discuss these questions with a partner. |

1. In the dialog, what was the communication problem?
2. Have you ever had a communication problem?
3. What chores might students do in a homestay?

Passage

Pairwork Student A and Student B have the same passage, but the gaps are different. Take turns reading the sentences aloud to your partner, and write the missing words in the gaps.

Student A

Host Family Rules

Every homestay is different. Some host families have a lot of rules, others do not. It is 1._____ to ask your host family about the rules. What are some typical rules?

First, you should help with chores in the house, such as 2._____ or clearing the table. You are responsible for cleaning your bedroom. Talk to your host family about when you can do your 3._____, and check about the best time to take a shower.

Always tell your host family what time you will come 4._____. It is important to be on time for meals. If you will be late or miss a meal, tell your host family in 5._____. Talk to them if you have any food allergies or serious dislikes. Also, ask your host family in advance if you want to bring a 6._____ home.

If you want to use the home telephone, check when you can use it. Also, learn the emergency 7._____ number for the police, ambulance or fire service.

Finally, you should behave as a family member, not as a guest. Talk to your host 8._____ about your needs or problems. If you are not sure about something, ask!

Pairwork — Student A and Student B have the same passage, but the gaps are different. Take turns reading the sentences aloud to your partner, and write the missing words in the gaps.

Student B

Host Family Rules

Every homestay is different. Some __1._____ families have a lot of rules, others do not. It is important to ask your host family about the rules. What are some typical __2._____?

First, you should help with chores in the house, such as setting or clearing the table. You are responsible for cleaning your __3._____. Talk to your host family about when you can do your laundry, and check about the best time to take a __4._____.

Always tell your host family what time you will come home. It is important to be on time for meals. If you will be __5._____ or miss a meal, tell your host family in advance. Talk to them if you have any food allergies or serious __6._____. Also, ask your host family in advance if you want to bring a friend home.

If you want to use the home telephone, __7._____ when you can use it. Also, learn the emergency telephone number for the police, ambulance or fire service.

Finally, you __8._____ behave as a family member, not as a guest. Talk to your host family about your needs or problems. If you are not sure about something, ask!

Each Host Family Is Different   Unit 3

Checking   Listen to the passage on the previous pages and check your answers.

Comprehension   Think about the passage, then answer the questions below.

1. Are all homestays the same?
   _____

2. Is the host family responsible for cleaning your bedroom?
   _____

3. Is it important to be on time for meals?
   _____

4. What should you do if you are going to be late for dinner?
   _____

5. What should you do if you want a friend to visit your homestay?
   _____

6. If you are not sure about something, what should you do?
   _____

Message from Junko

I had some communication problems with my host family, but I always tried to understand and solve each problem. After I solved the problems, I felt good. Solving them helped me to develop and become stronger.

Advice from Junko

Speaking with your host family every day is a good way to improve your English. Don't stay in your room all the time!

Useful Expressions

Phrases on the Topic Below are some useful phrases related to this unit. Check (✓) any ones that are difficult for you to understand.

At Home

1. ☐ I'm home. — ただいま。
2. ☐ How was your day? — 今日はどうでしたか。
3. ☐ May I use the computer? — コンピューターを使ってもよいですか。
4. ☐ Can you show me how to use the washing machine? — 洗濯機の使い方を教えてもらえますか。
5. ☐ There is no toilet paper. — トイレットペーパーがありません。
6. ☐ Where is the detergent? — 洗剤はどこですか。
7. ☐ I'll wash the dishes. — 私が洗い物をします。
8. ☐ Can I help? — 手伝いましょうか。
9. ☐ Let me help. — 手伝わせてください。
10. ☐ I'll be more careful in the future. — 今後はもっと気を付けます。
11. ☐ When is the best time for a shower? — シャワーを使うのに最適な時間はいつですか。
12. ☐ I'm sorry but I'm going to be late for dinner. — すみませんが、夕食に遅れます。
13. ☐ What is "meatloaf"? — 「ミートローフ」とは何ですか。
    ☐ — It's ground meat cooked in the shape of a loaf. — ひき肉をパン形に固めて焼いた料理です。
14. ☐ What's the emergency telephone number in the US? — アメリカでの緊急時の電話番号は何番ですか。
    ☐ — It's 9-1-1. — 911です。

Allergies

15. ☐ Are you allergic to anything? — 何かアレルギーがありますか。
    ☐ — I'm allergic to cats. — 猫アレルギーです。
16. ☐ Do you have any allergies? — 何かアレルギーがありますか。
    ☐ — I have an allergy to peanuts. — ピーナッツにアレルギーがあります。

Pronunciation Listen and repeat the phrases above. Say each one clearly.

Each Host Family Is Different   Unit 3

Numbers | Telephone

Below is some information about saying telephone numbers.

Example Numbers

123-456-7890	=	one-two-three, four-five-six, seven-eight-nine-zero
	=	one-two-three, four-five-six, seven-eight-nine-oh
(481) 655-2144	=	four-eight-one, six-five-five, two-one-four-four
	=	four-eight-one, six-double-five, two-one-double-four

Notes
- When you say a telephone number, read each number clearly.
- Do not read each hyphen "-" in a telephone number, but make a pause.
- You can say the number "0" as "zero" or "oh."
- You can say "double" if a number is repeated.

Emergency Numbers

| [US/Canada] | 911 | = | nine-one-one | [Australia] | 000 | = | triple-zero |
| [UK] | 999 | = | nine-nine-nine | [New Zealand] | 111 | = | one-one-one |

Notes
- In Japan, the emergency numbers for the police and fire department are different, but in each country above, there is just one number.
- You can say "triple" if a series of three numbers are the same.

Pronunciation Listen and repeat the following telephone numbers. Say each one clearly.

1. 745-9901
2. 911
3. 000
4. 625-932-0451
5. (177) 388-1271
6. 999
7. 111
8. 237-8943
9. (615) 402-2233
10. (380) 291-4398

33

Unit 4
I'm Experiencing Culture Shock

This unit is about cultural differences between Japan and other countries. There is also information about the stages of culture shock.

Warm-up ▶ Ask these questions to a partner.

1. Have you ever traveled overseas? If so, where?
2. Do you like living in Japan? Why or why not?
3. Would you like to live in another country for a long time? Why or why not?

Vocabulary

Keywords — Do you know the meanings of the words below? Check (✓) any ones that are difficult for you to understand.

1. ☐ adjustment [n] ▶ 調整、順応、適応
2. ☐ bicultural [adj] ▶ 2つの文化に対応できる
3. ☐ complain about [v] ▶ （物事）について不満を言う
4. ☐ cultural difference [n] ▶ 文化の違い
5. ☐ culture shock [n] ▶ カルチャーショック
6. ☐ experience [n] ▶ 経験
7. ☐ kid [v] ▶ 冗談を言う
8. ☐ overseas [adv] ▶ 海外で／に／へ
9. ☐ stage [n] ▶ 段階
10. ☐ tourist [n] ▶ 観光客

Pronunciation — Listen and repeat the words above. Say each one clearly.

Unit 4 — I'm Experiencing Culture Shock

Definitions — Match each word in the box to the best definition below. The first one has been done for you.

| adjustment | bicultural | complain about | cultural difference | culture shock |
| experience | kid | overseas | stage | tourist |

1. _culture shock_ — the confusion felt by someone who moves to a new place
2. _____ — abroad, another country across the sea
3. _____ — someone who travels for enjoyment
4. _____ — something that happens to you
5. _____ — to say something is wrong or you do not like it
6. _____ — a way of thinking or living that is not the same in each country
7. _____ — a small change for the better
8. _____ — to say something as a joke
9. _____ — understanding the feelings and customs of two cultures
10. _____ — a step, a level

Extra: The prefix "bi-" at the start of a word means "two." Here are some examples: a "bicycle" has two wheels; a "bilingual" person can speak two languages; and a "bicultural" person understands two cultures.

Dialog

Listening — Min is another international student. Junko is visiting Min's host family's house. Listen to the dialog, then answer the questions below.

1. What is Junko holding?

2. What does Junko not like?

3. How long has Junko been in the US?

Speaking Listen to the dialog again and read along. Then, read it aloud with a partner several times. Each time you read, change the underlined words (1–4) using the table below.

Min: Hey, Junko, what are you doing?

Junko: I'm ¹visiting your room.

Min: No, I mean why are you holding your shoes?

Junko: I always take off my shoes in the house.

Min: What? ² Are you kidding? We're in America now. It's OK to wear shoes inside the house.

Junko: Well, I don't like it. It feels really dirty.

Min: That's because you haven't been here long. When did you arrive?

Junko: ³ A couple of weeks ago.

Min: Well, you'll get used to it after a month or two.

Junko: Really?

Min: Sure. It's not ⁴ bad. It's just different.

Junko: OK, I see.

1	2	3	4
meeting you	Are you joking?	Several weeks	wrong
visiting you	Are you for real?	A short time	strange
talking with you	Are you serious?	A few weeks	weird

Discussion Think about the dialog above, then discuss these questions with a partner.

1. In the dialog, what was the cultural difference?
2. What are some other cultural differences between Japan and the US?
3. Have you ever experienced culture shock? If so, when?

Passage

Pairwork Student A and Student B have the same passage, but the gaps are different. Take turns reading the sentences aloud to your partner, and write the missing words in the gaps.

Student A

Stages of Culture Shock

Most people experience the same stages when they go to a new culture. First, everything feels new and ¹_____. This is the "honeymoon stage," and it might last for one week or a few weeks. It is also called the "tourist stage."

Second, after the "honeymoon stage" comes the "stress stage." Daily things, such as ²_____, transportation, and language are different, so you feel stressed. Problems seem more ³_____, and many things seem dirty or unhealthy. You may feel confused, lonely or angry. Also, you may ⁴_____ about the new culture and might want to return home.

The third stage is the "adjustment ⁵_____." Now you make more friends and learn more language. In this stage, you slowly become more positive and learn to live with cultural ⁶_____. Your experiences help you to grow and you may start to become bicultural.

Finally, when you return to your home country, you experience "re-entry ⁷_____." During your stay abroad you have changed. However, your friends and family in Japan have not shared your experiences, so you may feel like a stranger in your own ⁸_____.

Pairwork — Student A and Student B have the same passage, but the gaps are different. Take turns reading the sentences aloud to your partner, and write the missing words in the gaps.

Student B

Stages of Culture Shock

Most people experience the same stages when they go to a new ¹_____. First, everything feels new and exciting. This is the "honeymoon stage," and it might last for one week or a few weeks. It is also called the "²_____ stage."

Second, after the "honeymoon stage" comes the "stress stage." Daily things, such as food, transportation, and language are different, so you ³_____ stressed. Problems seem more difficult, and many things seem ⁴_____ or unhealthy. You may feel confused, lonely or angry. Also, you may complain about the new culture and might want to return ⁵_____.

The third stage is the "adjustment stage." Now you make more friends and learn more language. In this stage, you slowly become more ⁶_____ and learn to live with cultural differences. Your experiences help you to grow and you may start to become ⁷_____.

Finally, when you return to your home country, you experience "re-entry shock." During your stay abroad you have changed. However, your friends and ⁸_____ in Japan have not shared your experiences, so you may feel like a stranger in your own country.

I'm Experiencing Culture Shock | Unit 4

Checking Listen to the passage on the previous pages and check your answers.

Comprehension Think about the passage, then answer the questions below.

1. Do most people go through the same culture shock stages?
   _____

2. What is the name of the first stage when everything is positive?
   _____

3. How long does the first stage last?
   _____

4. How may you feel in the "stress stage"?
   _____

5. In which stage do you learn to live with cultural differences?
   _____

6. What problems might you have when you return to your own country?
   _____

Message from Junko

When I arrived in America, everything was great. That was my honeymoon stage. But after a couple of weeks, I became stressed about small things. Then I suffered from culture shock. Later, I adjusted and became open to cultural differences. Finally I understood that each country is different, and differences can be beautiful.

Advice from Junko

It is good to be flexible and open to new experiences!

39

Useful Expressions

Phrases on the Topic Below are some useful phrases related to this unit. Check (✓) any ones that are difficult for you to understand.

Culture Shock

1. ☐ The honeymoon stage is very enjoyable. ハネムーン段階はとても楽しいです。
2. ☐ My friend complains about everything. 私の友人は何にでも不満を言います。
3. ☐ I am now experiencing culture shock. 今、カルチャーショックを体験しています。
4. ☐ Finally I got used to life in America. 最終的にはアメリカの生活に慣れました。
5. ☐ I adjusted to life in Australia. オーストラリアの生活に適応しました。

Feelings/Problems

6.
   - ☐ How are you feeling? 気分はどうですか。
   - ☐ — I am excited. わくわくしています。
   - ☐ — Everything is exciting. 何もかもが刺激的です。
   - ☐ — I miss Japanese food. 日本食が恋しいです。
   - ☐ — I get annoyed about small things. 小さなことにいらいらします。
7. ☐ What should I do about this problem? どのようにこの問題に対処したらよいですか。

Experiences

8. ☐ Be open to new experiences! 新しい経験を受け入れましょう。
9. ☐ I want to experience a homestay. ホームステイを体験したいです。
10. ☐ I'd like to make a lot of friends. たくさんの友人を作りたいです。
11. ☐ I want to go sightseeing in the UK. イギリスで観光に行きたいです。
12. ☐ I had some great experiences. 素晴らしい体験をしました。

Time

13.
    - ☐ How long are you going to stay in New Zealand? どのくらいニュージーランドに滞在する予定ですか。
    - ☐ — I'm going to stay for a half year. 半年間滞在するつもりです。
14.
    - ☐ How long is your study abroad? 留学期間はどのくらいですか。
    - ☐ — It's three months. 3か月です。

Pronunciation Listen and repeat the phrases above. Say each one clearly.

I'm Experiencing Culture Shock | Unit 4

Numbers — Dates

Below is some information about saying dates.

Days of the Month

1st	=	first	11th	=	eleventh	21st	=	twenty first	31st = thirty first
2nd	=	second	12th	=	twelfth	22nd	=	twenty second	
3rd	=	third	13th	=	thirteenth	23rd	=	twenty third	
4th	=	fourth	14th	=	fourteenth	24th	=	twenty fourth	
5th	=	fifth	15th	=	fifteenth	25th	=	twenty fifth	
6th	=	sixth	16th	=	sixteenth	26th	=	twenty sixth	
7th	=	seventh	17th	=	seventeenth	27th	=	twenty seventh	
8th	=	eighth	18th	=	eighteenth	28th	=	twenty eighth	
9th	=	ninth	19th	=	nineteenth	29th	=	twenty ninth	
10th	=	tenth	20th	=	twentieth	30th	=	thirtieth	

Notes

▸ The pronunciation of "13th" and "30th" is similar, so be careful.
▸ Dates are written differently in different countries. For example, "August 17th" in the US is "17th August" in the UK.
▸ These numbers ("first," "second" and so on) are also used for ranking and lists.

Pronunciation Listen and repeat the following dates. Say each one clearly.

1. April 1st
2. July 30th
3. October 31st
4. January 20th
5. February 23rd
6. November 22nd
7. August 8th
8. June 12th
9. March 13th
10. December 25th

41

Unit 5 — My Dormitory Is too Noisy

This unit is about living in a dormitory. There are also some useful phrases for making suggestions and requests.

Warm-up ▶ Ask these questions to a partner.

1. Do you live in a house, apartment or dormitory?
2. Do you like it? Why or why not?
3. Who do you live with?

Vocabulary

Keywords Do you know the meanings of the words below? Check (✓) any ones that are difficult for you to understand.

1. ☐ assertive [adj]   ▶ 積極的な、自己主張が強い
2. ☐ convenient [adj]   ▶ 便利な、使いやすい
3. ☐ dawn [n]   ▶ 夜明け
4. ☐ dormitory [n]   ▶ 寮、寄宿舎
5. ☐ flexible [adj]   ▶ 柔軟な、適応性のある
6. ☐ lend [v]   ▶ 貸す
7. ☐ microwave oven [n] ▶ 電子レンジ
8. ☐ privacy [n]   ▶ プライバシー、私生活
9. ☐ refrigerator [n]   ▶ 冷蔵庫
10. ☐ roommate [n]   ▶ ルームメイト、同室者

Pronunciation Listen and repeat the words above. Say each one clearly.

My Dormitory Is too Noisy | Unit 5

Definitions

Match each word in the box to the best definition below. The first one has been done for you.

| assertive | convenient | dawn | dormitory | flexible |
| lend | microwave oven | privacy | refrigerator | roommate |

1. _____privacy_____ being alone where other people cannot see or hear you
2. _____ easy to use, easy to get to
3. _____ a person who lives in the same room as you
4. _____ early morning when the sky becomes light
5. _____ a machine that keeps food cold, also called a "fridge"
6. _____ able to change easily in different situations
7. _____ to give something to someone for a period of time
8. _____ an electric machine that cooks food quickly
9. _____ having a positive personality and saying what you think
10. _____ a building with bedrooms for a lot of people

Extra

The suffix "-ent" is a common ending for adjectives. For example, "convenient," "excellent," "different" and "independent." Changing the suffix to "-ence" makes the nouns: "convenience," "excellence," "difference" and "independence."

Dialog

Listening

Junko is going to class, and is talking with another international student, Omar. Listen to the dialog, then answer the questions below.

23

1. Is Omar ready for the test?

   _____

2. Did Omar sleep well?

   _____

3. What time did the party finish?

   _____

Speaking Listen to the dialog again and read along. Then, read it aloud with a partner several times. Each time you read, change the underlined words (1–4) using the table below.

Junko: Hi. Are you ready for the test?
Omar: Uh, no.
Junko: No? Omar, you look [1]tired. What's wrong?
Omar: I couldn't sleep last night.
Junko: Why not?
Omar: There was a really loud party in my dormitory. It went on until [2]2 o'clock.
Junko: Did you say anything about it?
Omar: No. The students in my dormitory are my friends. But they're always having parties!
Junko: I think you should be more assertive. [3]You should tell the dormitory staff.
Omar: Tell them what?
Junko: Say that you need some quiet time so that you can study or sleep.
Omar: OK, Junko, I guess you're right. [4]I'll talk to them later.

1	2	3	4
sleepy	midnight	You ought to	I'll contact them
pale	about 3 o'clock	I think you should	I'll speak with them
sick	dawn	You'd better	I'll tell them

Discussion Think about the dialog above, then discuss these questions with a partner.

1. In the dialog, what advice did Junko give Omar?
2. Do you like going to parties?
3. Have you ever suffered from a noise problem?

Passage

Pairwork Student A and Student B have the same passage, but the gaps are different. Take turns reading the sentences aloud to your partner, and write the missing words in the gaps.

Student A

Dormitory Life

A dormitory, or a "dorm," is a large building where people, often students, live. Dormitories are popular with students because they are not very
1._____. Also, they are often in a convenient location near the university campus. Therefore, you can walk to the classrooms, sports
2._____ and cafeterias.

Students in a dormitory share a room with roommates or they have their own private rooms. There are TV lounges, 3._____ machines and showers for everyone to use. There may be kitchens where students can cook, with stoves, refrigerators and 4._____ ovens.

Dormitories can be a good place to make friends. It may be fun to cook meals together in the 5._____ areas. However, do not tell too much personal information to other students until you know them well. Also, you should be careful about lending 6._____ or cellphones to other people.

Many students are living together so there are often interesting activities or parties. However, some
7._____ are noisy, and it might be difficult to get privacy. Try to be flexible and positive. If you have any problems, be
8._____ and tell the dormitory staff!

Pairwork — Student A and Student B have the same passage, but the gaps are different. Take turns reading the sentences aloud to your partner, and write the missing words in the gaps.

Student B

Dormitory Life

A dormitory, or a "dorm," is a large ¹_____ where people, often students, live. Dormitories are popular with students because they are not very expensive. Also, they are often in a convenient location near the university ²_____. Therefore you can walk to the classrooms, sports gyms and cafeterias.

Students in a dormitory share a room with ³_____ or they have their own private rooms. There are TV lounges, laundry machines and showers for everyone to use. There may be ⁴_____ where students can cook, with stoves, refrigerators and microwave ovens.

Dormitories can be a good place to make ⁵_____. It may be fun to cook meals together in the kitchen areas. However, do not tell too much personal information to other ⁶_____ until you know them well. Also, you should be careful about lending money or cellphones to other people.

Many students are ⁷_____ together so there are often interesting activities or parties. However, some dormitories are noisy, and it might be difficult to get ⁸_____. Try to be flexible and positive. If you have any problems, be assertive and tell the dormitory staff!

My Dormitory Is too Noisy — Unit 5

Checking — Listen to the passage on the previous pages and check your answers.

Comprehension — Think about the passage, then answer the questions below.

1. What is a "dorm"?
   _____

2. Why are dormitories popular with students?
   _____

3. Do all students have private rooms?
   _____

4. What are three things that dormitories have for everyone to use?
   _____

5. What should you be careful about doing?
   _____

6. What should you do if you have a problem?
   _____

Message from Junko
Omar spoke to the dormitory staff about the noise problem, and later he moved to another dormitory. The new dormitory was much quieter and better for him.

Advice from Junko
It is important to tell other people what you are thinking. If there is a problem and you don't speak, other people will not understand. Don't be passive. Be assertive!

47

Useful Expressions

Phrases on the Topic — Below are some useful phrases related to this unit. Check (✓) any ones that are difficult for you to understand.

Suggestions/Responses

1. ☐ We should clean up this room. 私たちはこの部屋を片付けるべきです。
2. ☐ Let's cook dinner together. 一緒に夕食を作りましょう。
   ☐ — Sure, let's do that. もちろん、そうしましょう。
3. ☐ Shall we have a party tonight? 今夜パーティをしましょうか。
   ☐ — That sounds good. それはいいですね。
4. ☐ Why don't we go shopping? 買い物に行きませんか。
   ☐ — I'm sorry, but I'm really busy. すみませんが、とても忙しいのです。
5. ☐ Would you like to go out to eat? 食事をしに出かけませんか。
   ☐ — Unfortunately, I have an assignment. 残念ですが、宿題があるのです。

Requests

6. ☐ Can I have some sugar? 砂糖をもらえますか。
7. ☐ Can I borrow your stapler? あなたのホッチキスを借りてもよいですか。
8. ☐ Can you lend me your dictionary? あなたの辞書を貸してもらえますか。
9. ☐ Can you tell me how to use the microwave oven? 電子レンジの使い方を教えてもらえますか。
10. ☐ Could you please be quieter? もう少し静かにしていただけますか。
11. ☐ Could you pass me the plate? そのお皿を渡していただけますか。
12. ☐ Could you give me a hand? 手伝っていただけますか。
13. ☐ Please knock on the door before you come in. 入室前にドアをノックしてください。

Clarifying

14. ☐ What do you mean? どういう意味ですか。
15. ☐ Can you say that again? もう一度言ってもらえますか。
16. ☐ Could you speak a bit slower, please? もう少しゆっくり話していただけますか。

Pronunciation — Listen and repeat the phrases above. Say each one clearly.

My Dormitory Is too Noisy | Unit 5

Numbers | Size

Below are two systems for measuring size: the metric and customary systems. Japan uses the metric system, but the US uses the customary system.

Metric System

millimeter (mm)
centimeter (cm) → 1 cm = 10 mm
meter (m) → 1 m = 100 cm = 1,000 mm

Useful Conversions

1 m = 39.4 in
1 m = 3 ft 3.4 in

Customary System

inch (in)
foot/feet (ft) → 1 ft = 12 in
yard (yd) → 1 yd = 3 ft = 36 in

Useful Conversions

1 in = 2.54 cm
1 ft = 30.5 cm

> **Notes**
> ▸ In the customary system, 1 foot is sometimes written as 1', and 1 inch is 1". So 11' 8" is 11 ft 8 in.
> ▸ Also, "foot" is the single form and "feet" is the plural form. So we say "1 foot" and "2 feet."
> ▸ The spelling of some words is different in different countries. For example, the spelling is "meter" in the US and "metre" in the UK.
> ▸ In the UK, the customary system is called the "imperial system."

Pronunciation Listen and repeat the following sizes. Say each one clearly.

1. 5 mm
2. 1 ft
3. 2 ft
4. 115 cm
5. 45 in
6. 1 m 55 cm
7. 5 ft 1 in
8. 15' 8"
9. about 5 m
10. 22 yd

Unit 6

How Can I Make Friends?

This unit is about making friends with people from other countries. There is also information about activities you can do overseas.

Warm-up ▶ Ask these questions to a partner.

1. Do you have any foreign friends now?
2. What are some good points about having foreign friends?
3. If you stay abroad for a month, what things do you want to do with your foreign friends?

Vocabulary

Keywords Do you know the meanings of the words below? Check (✓) any ones that are difficult for you to understand.

1. ☐ activity [n] ▶ 活動
2. ☐ available [adj] ▶ (利用や入手が)可能な
3. ☐ be interested in [v+adj] ▶ (物事)に関心がある
4. ☐ borrow [v] ▶ 借りる
5. ☐ fascinating [adj] ▶ とても興味深い
6. ☐ go sightseeing [v+n] ▶ 観光に行く
7. ☐ join a gym [v+n] ▶ スポーツクラブに入る
8. ☐ opportunity [n] ▶ 機会、好機
9. ☐ participate in [v] ▶ (活動など)に参加する
10. ☐ reduce stress [v+n] ▶ ストレスを減らす

Pronunciation Listen and repeat the words above. Say each one clearly.

Unit 6 — How Can I Make Friends?

Definitions

Match each word in the box to the best definition below. The first one has been done for you.

| activity | available | be interested in | borrow | fascinating |
| go sightseeing | join a gym | opportunity | participate in | reduce stress |

1. __be interested in__ — to like something, to want to know more about something
2. _____ — to visit places that are interesting, beautiful or famous
3. _____ — a chance
4. _____ — to become a member of a sports club
5. _____ — very interesting
6. _____ — to get something and keep it for a period of time
7. _____ — to take part in something, to do something with other people
8. _____ — possible to use or get
9. _____ — to remove a feeling of worry or tension
10. _____ — something that you do to have fun or relax

Extra

For a lot of activities, we use "go" plus the "-ing" form of the verb. For example: "go hiking," "go horseback riding," "go sightseeing," "go skiing," "go snowboarding," "go surfing" and "go swimming."

Dialog

Listening

Junko is at the university, and meets another international student, Sophie, for the first time. Listen to the dialog, then answer the questions below.

1. Where is Sophie from?

2. What is Junko reading?

3. What will Sophie and Junko do next?

Speaking Listen to the dialog again and read along. Then, read it aloud with a partner several times. Each time you read, change the underlined words (1–4) using the table below.

Sophie: Hi, I'm Sophie. What's your name?
Junko: I'm Junko. ¹Nice to meet you, Sophie.
Sophie: And you, Junko. Where are you from?
Junko: I'm from Japan. How about you?
Sophie: I'm from ²Greece. I came here last week. By the way, what are you reading?
Junko: Oh, it's a book about ³history.
Sophie: Is it interesting?
Junko: Yeah, it's fascinating. I borrowed it from the library yesterday.
Sophie: Really? I haven't been to the library yet. Where is it?
Junko: It's not far. I can take you there, if you like.
Sophie: ⁴Sure, let's go!

1	2	3	4
Good to meet you	France	art	That'll be great!
It's a pleasure to meet you	Germany	politics	Yeah, please!
Glad to meet you	Sweden	culture	I'd love to go!

Discussion Think about the dialog above, then discuss these questions with a partner.

1. In the dialog, where did Junko get the book?
2. Do you like reading books? If so, what kind?
3. What activities do you do in your free time?

Passage

Pairwork Student A and Student B have the same passage, but the gaps are different. Take turns reading the sentences aloud to your partner, and write the missing words in the gaps.

Student A

Activities Overseas

There are many different activities that you can enjoy overseas. You can continue doing your 1._____ or you can try something new.

One idea is to join a sports club. You may be able to 2._____ a university gym cheaply using your student card. Check what activities are available, and choose the ones that interest you. Doing 3._____ like volleyball, swimming or yoga is a good way to reduce stress.

Another idea is to go to sports events. For example, you can see 4._____, basketball or American football in the US. You can go to a soccer match in the UK. Or you can 5._____ cricket and rugby in New Zealand and Australia.

Many students take the opportunity to go sightseeing. Are you interested in nature, history, tall 6._____ or beautiful views? Being abroad is a great opportunity to visit famous places.

Finally, your university may organize regular activities such as 7._____ clubs or trips to interesting places. You can meet students from other countries if you participate in these activities. So you can practice English and make 8._____ at the same time!

Pairwork — Student A and Student B have the same passage, but the gaps are different. Take turns reading the sentences aloud to your partner, and write the missing words in the gaps.

Student B

Activities Overseas

There are many different ^{1.}_____ that you can enjoy overseas. You can continue doing your hobbies or you can try something new.

One ^{2.}_____ is to join a sports club. You may be able to join a university gym cheaply using your student card. Check what activities are ^{3.}_____, and choose the ones that interest you. Doing sports like volleyball, swimming or yoga is a good way to reduce ^{4.}_____.

Another idea is to go to sports events. For example, you can see baseball, basketball or American football in the US. You can ^{5.}_____ to a soccer match in the UK. Or you can watch cricket and rugby in New Zealand and Australia.

Many students take the ^{6.}_____ to go sightseeing. Are you interested in nature, history, tall buildings or beautiful views? Being abroad is a great opportunity to visit ^{7.}_____ places.

Finally, your university may organize regular activities such as conversation clubs or trips to interesting places. You can meet students from other countries if you ^{8.}_____ in these activities. So you can practice English and make friends at the same time!

How Can I Make Friends? | Unit 6

Checking — Listen to the passage on the previous pages and check your answers.

Comprehension — Think about the passage, then answer the questions below.

1. Are there many different activities to do overseas?
   _____

2. What is a good way to reduce stress?
   _____

3. What sports can you see in the US?
   _____

4. What sports can you watch in New Zealand and Australia?
   _____

5. Do many students go sightseeing?
   _____

6. How can you meet students from other countries?
   _____

Message from Junko

I took Sophie to the library. Later, we talked a lot and became good friends. I really enjoyed speaking English with her.

Advice from Junko

Don't spend all your time overseas with Japanese students. Be active and positive. Try to make friends with students from other countries!

55

Useful Expressions

Phrases on the Topic — Below are some useful phrases related to this unit. Check (✓) any ones that are difficult for you to understand.

Places

1. ☐ I'm lost. — 道に迷いました。
2. ☐ Where is the lost and found? — 遺失物取扱所はどこですか。
   ☐ — It's over there. — あちらです。
3. ☐ Where is the nearest bank? — 一番近い銀行はどこですか。
   ☐ — It's a couple of blocks away. — 2ブロックほど先です。
   ☐ — I can show you the way. — 行き方を説明しましょう。
4. ☐ Do you want to go sightseeing? — 観光に行きたいですか。
   ☐ — Yes, I'd love to see the Grand Canyon! — はい、是非グランドキャニオンを見たいです。
5. ☐ Have you been to the museum? — 博物館にはもう行きましたか。
   ☐ — Yes, it was pretty good. — はい、かなり良かったです。
6. ☐ Have you been to a Chinese restaurant here? — この辺の中華料理店にはもう行きましたか。
   ☐ — No, not yet. — いいえ、まだです。

Interests/Activities

7. ☐ Are you interested in music? — 音楽に関心がありますか。
   ☐ — Yes, I am. — はい、あります。
   ☐ — No, not really. — いいえ、そうでもありません。
8. ☐ What activities do you want to participate in? — どんな活動に参加したいですか。
   ☐ — I want to participate in university trips. — 大学主催の旅行に参加したいです。
9. ☐ I want to join a gym. — スポーツクラブに入会したいです。
10. ☐ I want to see an ice hockey game. — アイスホッケーの試合を観戦したいです。
11. ☐ A good way to reduce stress is to go jogging. — ストレスを減らす良い方法はジョギングをすることです。
12. ☐ I'm going out to eat with my new friends today. — 今日は新しい友達と食事に出かける予定です。

Pronunciation — Listen and repeat the phrases above. Say each one clearly.

How Can I Make Friends? | Unit 6

Numbers | Volume

Below are two systems for measuring liquid volumes: the metric and customary systems. Japan uses the metric system, but the US uses the customary system.

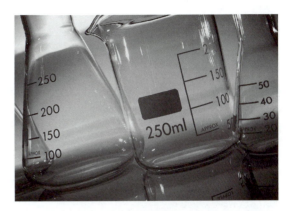

Metric System

milliliter (ml)
liter (L)   →   1 L = 1,000 ml

Customary System

pint
quart   →   1 quart = 2 pints
gallon →   1 gallon = 4 quarts = 8 pints

Useful Conversions

[US]   1 L = 2.11 pints   1 pint = 473 ml   1 quart = 946 ml   1 gallon = 3.79 L
[UK]   1 L = 1.76 pints   1 pint = 568 ml   1 quart = 1.14 L   1 gallon = 4.55 L

Notes

▸ The spelling of some words is different in different countries. For example, the spelling is "liter" in the US and "litre" in the UK.
▸ The size of a pint, a quart and a gallon is different in the US and the UK. For example, in the US 1 pint is 473 milliliters, but in the UK 1 pint is 568 millilitres.
▸ In the UK, the customary system is called the "imperial system."

Pronunciation

Listen and repeat the following volumes. Say each one clearly.

1. 2 L
2. 3 pints
3. 250 ml
4. 4.5 L
5. half a gallon
6. 2 quarts
7. 355 ml
8. about 10 gallons
9. 500 ml
10. about 700 L

Review of Units 1–6

This is a review of the Keywords, Phrases on the Topic and Numbers sections in Units 1–6.

Keywords

Do you remember the Keywords from Units 1–6? Write the correct English words below.

1. 搭乗券
2. 預ける手荷物
3. 機内に持ち込む鞄
4. 時差ボケ
5. 症状
6. 頭痛がする
7. 家事
8. アレルギーがある
9. （物事）に責任を持つ
10. 洗濯をする
11. 海外で／に／へ
12. 経験
13. 文化の違い
14. 積極的な、自己主張が強い
15. 便利な、使いやすい
16. 柔軟な、適応性のある
17. プライバシー、私生活
18. （活動など）に参加する
19. 機会、好機
20. 活動

Phrases on the Topic

A Do you remember the Phrases on the Topic from Units 1–6? Write the correct English phrases below.

1. あなたのスーツケースの重さはどれくらいですか。

2. (あなたは)超過手荷物料金を支払わなければなりません。

3. 喫煙は禁止されています。

4. 現地は何時ですか。

5. 私は時差ボケしています。

6. (私は)疲れています。

7. (私は)喉が痛いです。

8. 今日はどうでしたか。

9. (私は)ピーナッツにアレルギーがあります。

10. トイレットペーパーがありません。

11. (私は)半年間滞在するつもりです。

12. (私は)たくさんの友人を作りたいです。

13. （私は）今、カルチャーショックを体験しています。

14. （私は）日本食が恋しいです。

15. 手伝っていただけますか。

16. 私たちはこの部屋を片付けるべきです。

17. すみませんが、（私は）とても忙しいのです。

18. 遺失物取扱所はどこですか。

19. （あなたは）博物館にはもう行きましたか。

20. （あなたは）音楽に興味はありますか。

B The phrases below use some new words to review the Phrases on the Topic in Units 1–6. Read them aloud. Say each one clearly.

1. Do you have a window seat?
2. Your carry-on bag is overweight.
3. I have one suitcase to check in.
4. Japan is eight hours ahead of here.
5. I have a sore neck.
6. Los Angeles is 16 hours behind Japan.
7. I slept badly.
8. Can you show me how to use the dishwasher?
9. Are you allergic to seafood?
10. I'll wash the cups and glasses.
11. How long are you going to stay in the US?

12. I had some interesting experiences.
13. I'm going to stay for a couple of months.
14. I want to go sightseeing in California.
15. Let's make lunch together.
16. Can you tell me how to use the vacuum cleaner?
17. Could you pass me the cups?
18. Where is the bank?
19. Are you interested in fashion?
20. I'm going shopping with my new friends today.

Numbers

The phrases below review the Numbers sections in Units 1–6. Read them aloud. Say each one clearly.

1. My weight is 55 kg.
2. I weigh 135 lb.
3. This suitcase weighs about 20 kg.
4. We need 200 g of butter.
5. I bought about 3 lb of apples.
6. The class starts at 10:10 a.m.
7. I usually wake up at 7:15 a.m.
8. The departure time is 15:45.
9. Do you want to meet at the restaurant at 6:30 p.m.?
10. The phone number for the restaurant is (250) 739-5522.
11. The emergency phone number in the US is 911.
12. Her birthday is February 20th.
13. Christmas Day is December 25th.
14. What do you usually do on January 1st?
15. I am 1 m 60 cm tall.
16. Her height is 5 ft 3 in.
17. This is a 12" frying pan.
18. Let's buy 2 L of milk.
19. We should put about 800 ml of water in the curry.
20. This bottle contains 2 pints.

Unit 7
What Should I Talk About?

This unit is about talking with people from other countries. There are ideas for conversation topics and useful phrases for starting a conversation.

Warm-up ▶ Ask these questions to a partner.

1. How often do you speak English?
2. If you stay abroad for a month, what are good topics to talk about with foreign friends?
3. What are not good topics? Why not?

Vocabulary

Keywords — Do you know the meanings of the words below? Check (✓) any ones that are difficult for you to understand.

1. ☐ festival [n] ▶ 祝祭、祭り
2. ☐ follow advice [v+n] ▶ アドバイスに従う
3. ☐ frustrating [adj] ▶ いら立たしい、もどかしい
4. ☐ national holiday [n] ▶ 国民の祝日
5. ☐ personal information [n] ▶ 個人情報
6. ☐ politics [n] ▶ 政治
7. ☐ race [n] ▶ 人種
8. ☐ religion [n] ▶ 宗教
9. ☐ taboo [n] ▶ タブー、禁物、禁句
10. ☐ topic [n] ▶ 話題

Pronunciation — Listen and repeat the words above. Say each one clearly.

Unit 7 — What Should I Talk About?

Definitions Match each word in the box to the best definition below. The first one has been done for you.

> festival   follow advice   ~~frustrating~~   national holiday   personal information
> politics   race   religion   taboo   topic

1. ___frustrating___ — making you stressed when you cannot do what you want to do
2. _____ — for example, Christianity, Islam, Buddhism or Hinduism
3. _____ — a special day when most people do not go to work or school
4. _____ — a subject that you talk about or write about
5. _____ — to do as someone suggests
6. _____ — details about a person such as age, address and medical history
7. _____ — a special time or period when people celebrate
8. _____ — the activity of controlling a country
9. _____ — something you should not say or do
10. _____ — a group of people sharing the same history, culture or language

Extra To "follow advice" means to do what another person suggests. For example, "I follow my teacher's advice and I speak a lot of English every day." We also say "follow directions," "follow instructions" and "follow orders."

Dialog

Listening Junko is at the university campus, and is talking with another international student, Wei. Listen to the dialog, then answer the questions below. 🎧 33

1. Is Wei happy?

2. What question does Wei's host mother ask her?

3. Can Wei answer the question?

Speaking Listen to the dialog again and read along. Then, read it aloud with a partner several times. Each time you read, change the underlined words (1–4) using the table below.

Junko: Hey, Wei. ¹How are you doing?

Wei: Not so good.

Junko: What's the problem?

Wei: Every evening my host mother asks me the same question. She says, "How was your day?"

Junko: So?

Wei: I don't know ²what to say. It's really frustrating!

Junko: Well, you can talk about many things. For example, ³your classes and your friends.

Wei: Oh, I see.

Junko: Also, it's good if you ask your host mother the same question.

Wei: What? Do you mean I should ask about her day?

Junko: Yes, sure.

Wei: OK, thanks. I'll ⁴try that.

1	2	3	4
How's it going?	how to reply	what you learned at school	follow your advice
How's everything?	what I should say	what you did after school	do that
How are things?	how to answer	your school activities	give that a go

Discussion Think about the dialog above, then discuss these questions with a partner.

1. In the dialog, what advice did Junko give Wei?
2. Yesterday, how was your day?
3. Today, how are you doing?

Passage

 Student A and Student B have the same passage, but the gaps are different. Take turns reading the sentences aloud to your partner, and write the missing words in the gaps.

Student A

Conversation Topics

Here is some advice to help you in conversations with your international friends or your host family.

One [1]_____ conversation topic is Japan. Some people want to hear about Japanese culture, such as food, festivals, music and famous places. Take [2]_____ from Japan with you on your trip. If you have pictures, it is easier to talk.

Also, you should ask questions about the country you are [3]_____. What are the best festivals? When are the national holidays? What is interesting about the culture?

Other good conversation topics include [4]_____, movies, music, fashion, shopping, sports and famous places. Learn English vocabulary for the topics you want to talk about. For example, [5]_____ words to describe your hobbies so that you can talk about them in English.

However, some topics might make people feel uncomfortable. Be careful when talking about [6]_____, religion, race or personal information. These topics may be taboo for some people.

Finally, do not worry if you do not understand something or if you [7]_____ a mistake. Try to keep talking, and ask questions if you do not understand. Asking questions is an important part of having a [8]_____!

Pairwork — Student A and Student B have the same passage, but the gaps are different. Take turns reading the sentences aloud to your partner, and write the missing words in the gaps.

Student B

Conversation Topics

Here is some ¹_____ to help you in conversations with your international friends or your host family.

One good conversation topic is Japan. Some people want to hear about Japanese ²_____, such as food, festivals, music and famous places. Take photographs from Japan with you on your trip. If you have pictures, it is easier to ³_____.

Also, you should ask questions about the country you are visiting. What are the best festivals? When are the national ⁴_____? What is interesting about the culture?

Other good conversation topics include hobbies, movies, music, fashion, shopping, sports and famous places. Learn English ⁵_____ for the topics you want to talk about. For example, learn words to describe your hobbies so that you can talk ⁶_____ them in English.

However, some topics might make people feel uncomfortable. Be careful when talking about politics, religion, race or personal information. These topics may be ⁷_____ for some people.

Finally, do not worry if you do not understand something or if you make a mistake. Try to keep talking, and ask questions if you do not ⁸_____. Asking questions is an important part of having a conversation!

| | What Should I Talk About? | Unit 7 |

Checking — Listen to the passage on the previous pages and check your answers.

Comprehension — Think about the passage, then answer the questions below.

1. To help you talk about Japan, what should you take on your trip?
   _____

2. Should you ask questions about the country you are visiting?
   _____

3. What are three good conversation topics?
   _____

4. Are all conversation topics good?
   _____

5. Which conversation topics should you be careful about?
   _____

6. What should you do when you do not understand?
   _____

Message from Junko
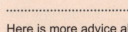
Wei tried hard to communicate with her host family. Every day, she prepared one or two topics to talk about. Slowly, it became easier for her to talk with them.

Advice from Junko
Here is more advice about communication: smile and use gestures. Remember, the best way to improve your English is to practice as much as possible. Speak, speak, speak!

Useful Expressions

Phrases on the Topic — Below are some useful phrases related to this unit. Check (✓) any ones that are difficult for you to understand.

Starting a Conversation

1. ☐ How are you doing? 調子はどうですか。
   ☐ — I'm great. とても良いです。
2. ☐ How's it going? 調子はどうですか。
   ☐ — It's all right. 順調です。
3. ☐ How was school? 学校はどうでしたか。
   ☐ — It was a lot of fun. とても楽しかったです。
4. ☐ What's up? 最近はどうですか。
5. ☐ Let's talk about movies. 映画について話しましょう。

Advice

6. ☐ I asked my friend for advice. 友人にアドバイスを求めました。
7. ☐ My friend gave me advice. 友人がアドバイスをくれました。
8. ☐ I followed my friend's advice. 友人のアドバイスに従いました。
9. ☐ I ignored my friend's advice. 友人のアドバイスを無視しました。

Culture

10. ☐ What is your favorite festival? あなたの好きな祭りは何ですか。
11. ☐ How do you celebrate New Year in your country? あなたの国では新年をどのように祝いますか。
12. ☐ What are the most important national holidays here? ここで最も重要な祝日は何ですか。
13. ☐ What do people enjoy doing here during summer? ここでは人々は、夏の間何をして楽しみますか。

Taboo Topics

14. ☐ That's a personal subject. それは個人的なことです。
15. ☐ Let's talk about something different. 何か他のことについて話しましょう。
16. ☐ Can we change the subject? 話題を変えてもよいですか。
17. ☐ I'd rather not talk about that. そのことについては話したくありません。

Pronunciation — Listen and repeat the phrases above. Say each one clearly.

Numbers 1–10,000

Below is some information about saying numbers from 1 to 10,000.

Basic Units

100	=	one hundred
1,000	=	one thousand
10,000	=	ten thousand

> **Notes**
> ▸ You can also say 100 and 1,000 as "a hundred" and "a thousand."
> ▸ The comma "," is important for large numbers in English. If there is one comma in the number, it means "thousand." So 3,000 is "three thousand."

Example Numbers

200	=	two hundred	1,500	=	one thousand five hundred
350	=	three hundred fifty	4,630	=	four thousand six hundred thirty
509	=	five hundred nine	6,022	=	six thousand twenty-two
712	=	seven hundred twelve	8,954	=	eight thousand nine hundred fifty-four

> **Notes**
> ▸ In British English, you say "and" after "hundred." For example, you say 350 as "three hundred and fifty" and 4,630 as "four thousand six hundred and thirty."
> ▸ In American English, you can read some "thousand" numbers using "hundred." For example, you can say 1,500 as "fifteen hundred" or 6,300 as "sixty-three hundred."

Pronunciation Listen and repeat the following numbers. Say each one clearly.

1. 330
2. 427
3. 699
4. 1,100
5. 3,572
6. about 5,000
7. 6,383
8. 8,455
9. 9,999
10. about 10,000

Unit 8

I Feel Homesick

This unit is about feeling homesick.
There is information about things that make you feel homesick and what you can do to feel better.

Warm-up ▶ Ask these questions to a partner.

1. What things do you most like about Japan?
2. Have you ever lived away from your family?
3. Do you like visiting new places?

Vocabulary

Keywords — Do you know the meanings of the words below? Check (✓) any ones that are difficult for you to understand.

1. ☐ achieve [v] ▶ 成し遂げる
2. ☐ comfortable [adj] ▶ 快適な、楽な
3. ☐ counselor [n] ▶ カウンセラー、相談役
4. ☐ deal with [v] ▶ （問題など）に対処する
5. ☐ feel depressed [v+adj] ▶ 気がふさぐ、憂鬱になる
6. ☐ homesickness [n] ▶ ホームシック、郷愁
7. ☐ look forward to [v] ▶ （物事）を楽しみにする
8. ☐ miss [v] ▶ （人や物事が）恋しい
9. ☐ regularly [adv] ▶ 規則正しく、定期的に
10. ☐ unfamiliar [adj] ▶ 不慣れな、見知らぬ

Pronunciation — Listen and repeat the words above. Say each one clearly.

Unit 8 — I Feel Homesick

Definitions Match each word in the box to the best definition below. The first one has been done for you.

| achieve | comfortable | counselor | deal with | ~~feel depressed~~ |
| homesickness | look forward to | miss | regularly | unfamiliar |

1. _feel depressed_ — to be unhappy, without much energy
2. _____ — feeling unhappy because you are away from home
3. _____ — to find an answer for a problem
4. _____ — to succeed in doing something
5. _____ — not known to you, not seen before
6. _____ — to feel happy or excited about something that is going to happen
7. _____ — a person whose job is giving help or advice
8. _____ — to feel sad about a person you cannot see or a thing you cannot have
9. _____ — often, at the same time each day or week
10. _____ — making you feel relaxed and not worried

Extra The suffix "-ness" is a common ending for nouns. For example, "happiness," "homesickness," "laziness," "loneliness" and "tiredness." Removing the suffix makes the adjectives: "happy," "homesick," "lazy," "lonely" and "tired."

Dialog

Listening Junko is in a cafeteria, and is talking with her friend, Carlos. Listen to the dialog, then answer the questions below.

1. Is Junko happy?

2. What does Junko want to eat?

3. What are Junko and Carlos going to do on the weekend?

Speaking Listen to the dialog again and read along. Then, read it aloud with a partner several times. Each time you read, change the underlined words (1–4) using the table below.

Carlos: Junko, you don't look happy. What's up?
Junko: I don't ¹want to study. I just want to stay in my room.
Carlos: ²Why?
Junko: I miss my family in Japan. I want to eat Japanese food. Most of all, I want to go shopping with my friends in my hometown.
Carlos: Really? Are you OK?
Junko: No. I'm feeling ³depressed.
Carlos: That's not good. Why don't we do something on the weekend?
Junko: Like what?
Carlos: Let's go ⁴to a Japanese restaurant.
Junko: OK.
Carlos: We can invite Omar and Sophie.
Junko: That sounds nice. Thanks, Carlos.

1	2	3	4
feel like talking	What's the problem?	sad	bicycle riding
want to do anything	How come?	low	shopping
have any energy	What happened?	unhappy	and see a movie

Discussion Think about the dialog above, then discuss these questions with a partner.

1. In the dialog, what did Junko miss?
2. Have you ever felt homesick? If so, when?
3. If you stay abroad for a long time, what might you miss?

Passage

Pairwork — Student A and Student B have the same passage, but the gaps are different. Take turns reading the sentences aloud to your partner, and write the missing words in the gaps.

Student A

Dealing with Homesickness

Some people feel homesick when they live away from home. Homesickness is a feeling of ¹._____ your home and family. It can happen at any time during your stay abroad.

Why do people feel homesick? Homesickness comes from ²._____ situations. Life in Japan is comfortable. It is easy for you to communicate, eat your favorite food, and use the ³._____ system. In another country, these things may be frustrating. It might be difficult to speak English, find food that you like, or use buses and trains. Shopping might also be ⁴._____ because the money is unfamiliar.

How can you deal with homesickness? First, it is good to talk about your feelings. Speak with your host family, friends or a ⁵._____. Second, meet your friends regularly and do fun activities together. For example, play sports or ⁶._____ in university activities every week. Also, make fun plans for the weekends or holidays so that you have some nice things to ⁷._____ forward to.

Finally, remember your reasons for living abroad. Use these reasons as motivation to stay positive, and to help you ⁸._____ what you want to do.

Pairwork — Student A and Student B have the same passage, but the gaps are different. Take turns reading the sentences aloud to your partner, and write the missing words in the gaps.

Student B

Dealing with Homesickness

Some people feel [1.] _____ when they live away from home. Homesickness is a feeling of missing your home and family. It can happen at any time during your [2.] _____ abroad.

Why do people feel homesick? Homesickness comes from unfamiliar situations. Life in Japan is [3.] _____. It is easy for you to communicate, eat your favorite food, and use the transport system. In another country, these things may be frustrating. It might be [4.] _____ to speak English, find food that you like, or use buses and trains. Shopping might also be frustrating because the money is unfamiliar.

How can you deal [5.] _____ homesickness? First, it is good to talk about your feelings. Speak with your host family, friends or a counselor. Second, meet your friends [6.] _____ and do fun activities together. For example, play sports or participate in university activities every week. Also, make fun [7.] _____ for the weekends or holidays so that you have some nice things to look forward to.

Finally, remember your reasons for living abroad. Use these [8.] _____ as motivation to stay positive, and to help you achieve what you want to do.

I Feel Homesick | Unit 8

Checking Listen to the passage on the previous pages and check your answers.

Comprehension Think about the passage, then answer the questions below.

1. What is homesickness?
   _____

2. When can homesickness happen?
   _____

3. What situations does homesickness come from?
   _____

4. What are three things that may be frustrating in another country?
   _____

5. If you feel homesick, is it good to talk with someone?
   _____

6. What should you do regularly?
   _____

Message from Junko

I met Carlos and my other friends regularly during my time abroad. When I felt low or homesick, they helped me. We planned many fun activities, so we always had things to look forward to.

Advice from Junko

Other countries are different from Japan, so don't expect everything to be easy and comfortable. If you have problems, talk to someone about your feelings!

Useful Expressions

Phrases on the Topic — Below are some useful phrases related to this unit. Check (✓) any ones that are difficult for you to understand.

Homesickness

1. ☐ I miss my friends. — 友人に会えなくてさみしいです。
2. ☐ I miss taking a hot bath. — 熱い風呂に入れなくて残念です。
3. ☐ I really want to eat sushi. — 寿司がすごく食べたいです。
4. ☐ I feel lonely. — 私は孤独です。
5. ☐ I wish I could go home. — 家に帰れたらよいのにと思います。

Problems

6. ☐ I'm suffering from tiredness. — 私は疲労で苦しんでいます。
7. ☐ I don't feel like studying. — 勉強する気になりません。
8. ☐ How can I deal with this problem? — どのようにこの問題に対処したらよいですか。
9. ☐ Can you give me some advice? — 私にアドバイスをもらえますか。

No Problems

10.
    - ☐ Are you having a nice time here? — ここで快適な時間を過ごしていますか。
    - ☐ — Yes, everything is fantastic! — はい、何もかもが素晴らしいです。
    - ☐ — Yeah, awesome! — ええ、最高です。

Goals

11. ☐ What do you want to achieve? — 何を成し遂げたいですか。
12.
    - ☐ What are your goals? — あなたの目標は何ですか。
    - ☐ — I'd like to improve my speaking skill. — スピーキング力を伸ばしたいです。
    - ☐ — I want to be able to speak English fluently. — 英語を流暢に話せるようになりたいです。
13.
    - ☐ Why are you studying English? — なぜ英語を勉強しているのですか。
    - ☐ — I want to use English at work. — 仕事で英語を使いたいからです。
14. ☐ What career do you want to have? — どんな職業に就きたいですか。
15. ☐ Good luck with your studies! — 勉強を頑張ってください。

Pronunciation — Listen and repeat the phrases above. Say each one clearly.

Numbers 10,000+

Below is some information about saying numbers larger than 10,000.

Basic Units

10,000	=	ten thousand	1,000,000	=	one million
100,000	=	one hundred thousand	1,000,000,000	=	one billion

Notes

- You can also say 100,000, 1,000,000 and 1,000,000,000 as "a hundred thousand," "a million" and "a billion."
- A comma "," is used to separate numbers for "thousand," "million" or "billion." So 1,002,003,000 is "one billion, two million, three thousand."

Example Numbers

62,917	=	sixty-two thousand nine hundred seventeen
345,000	=	three hundred forty-five thousand
2,750,000	=	two million, seven hundred fifty thousand
690,800,150	=	six hundred ninety million, eight hundred thousand, one hundred fifty
7,125,000,000	=	seven billion, one hundred twenty-five million

Notes

- There is no "s" ending for "hundred," "thousand," "million" and "billion" in these large numbers.
- In British English, you say "and" after "hundred." For example, you say 2,750,000 as "two million, seven hundred and fifty thousand."

Pronunciation

Listen and repeat the following numbers. Say each one clearly.

1. 10,870
2. 155,000
3. 8,406,000
4. 750,250
5. 126,427,130
6. 64,100,000
7. 1,252,000,000
8. about 320,000,000
9. about 400,000
10. 2,399,639,955

Unit 9: How Do I Order Food?

This unit is about ordering food in a restaurant. There is also information about tipping and different currencies around the world.

Warm-up ▶ Ask these questions to a partner.

1. What is your favorite foreign food?
2. How often do you eat foreign food?
3. Is there any food that you cannot eat?

Vocabulary

Keywords Do you know the meanings of the words below? Check (✓) any ones that are difficult for you to understand.

1. ☐ appetizer [n]   ▶ 前菜、アペタイザー
2. ☐ check [n]   ▶ 勘定書
3. ☐ currency [n]   ▶ 通貨
4. ☐ main course [n]   ▶ 主菜、メインディッシュ
5. ☐ order [v]   ▶ 注文する
6. ☐ PIN number [n]   ▶ 暗証番号
7. ☐ server [n]   ▶ 給仕人、ウェイター、ウェイトレス
8. ☐ service charge [n] ▶ サービス料
9. ☐ takeout [n]   ▶ 持ち帰り用の飲食物
10. ☐ tip [n]   ▶ チップ

Pronunciation Listen and repeat the words above. Say each one clearly.

Unit 9 — How Do I Order Food?

Definitions

Match each word in the box to the best definition below. The first one has been done for you.

| appetizer | check | currency | main course | order |
| PIN number | server | ~~service charge~~ | takeout | tip |

1. _service charge_ — extra money for a service that is added to the basic price
2. _____ — food that you buy in a restaurant but eat in a different place
3. _____ — a secret number that you use with a bank card or a credit card
4. _____ — to ask for food or drinks in a restaurant
5. _____ — the largest or most important part of a meal
6. _____ — extra money paid to someone who has given a service
7. _____ — a piece of paper that shows how much you must pay in a restaurant
8. _____ — the money that is used in a country
9. _____ — a starter, a small dish that you eat at the start of a meal
10. _____ — a person who brings food in a restaurant, also called a "waiter/waitress"

Extra: There are many differences between American English and British English. For example, a "check" in the US is a "bill" in the UK. Here are more examples: "French fries" (US) = "chips" (UK), "soda" (US) = "fizzy drink" (UK).

Dialog

Listening — Junko is in a restaurant, and is ordering some food. Listen to the dialog, then answer the questions below.

🎧 43

1. Is Junko ordering dinner?

   _____

2. What food does Junko order?

   _____

3. What drink does Junko ask for?

   _____

Speaking

Listen to the dialog again and read along. Then, read it aloud with a partner several times. Each time you read, change the underlined words (1–4) using the table below.

Server: ¹Are you ready to order?
Junko: Yes, I'd like some lunch.
Server: Would you like an appetizer?
Junko: I'll have ²chicken soup, please.
Server: What would you like for a main course?
Junko: I'd like a hamburger and French fries.
Server: OK.
Junko: With no onions on the hamburger, please.
Server: Sure. ³Would you like anything to drink?
Junko: ⁴Just water, please.
Server: Would you like anything else?
Junko: No thanks.

1	2	3	4
May I take your order?	a green salad	Can I get you a drink?	A coke
Would you like to order?	nachos	What would you like to drink?	Orange juice
Can I take your order?	chicken wings	Would you like to order a drink?	An iced tea

Discussion Think about the dialog above, then discuss these questions with a partner.

1. In the dialog, what did Junko not want on her hamburger?
2. What do you usually eat for lunch?
3. How much money does your lunch usually cost?

Passage

Pairwork — Student A and Student B have the same passage, but the gaps are different. Take turns reading the sentences aloud to your partner, and write the missing words in the gaps.

Student A

Paying in a Restaurant

There are different ways of paying for a meal in different countries. For example, at the end of a meal in ¹._____ or the United States you say, "Can I have the check, please?" However, in the United Kingdom you say, "Can I have the ²._____, please?"

Another difference is tipping. In the US and Canada, tipping is common in restaurants. If the service is good, a ³._____ tip is normal. If the service is excellent, some people pay 20%. If the service is poor, they ⁴._____ less.

In the UK, tips of 10% are common in restaurants. However, tipping is not common in ⁵._____ or New Zealand.

Tipping is not required for fast food restaurants, coffee shops or ordering takeout. Also, some restaurants add a service charge to the ⁶._____. You do not have to tip if there is a service charge.

Finally, if you want to pay with a credit card, check that the ⁷._____ accepts your card. In some places, when you use a credit card, you need your ⁸._____ number. So make sure you know it!

Pairwork — Student A and Student B have the same passage, but the gaps are different. Take turns reading the sentences aloud to your partner, and write the missing words in the gaps.

Student B

Paying in a Restaurant

There are different ways of paying for a ⁱ_____ in different countries. For example, at the end of a meal in Canada or the United States you say, "Can I have the check, ²_____?" However, in the United Kingdom you say, "Can I have the bill, please?"

Another difference is tipping. In the US and Canada, ³_____ is common in restaurants. If the service is good, a 15% tip is normal. If the service is ⁴_____, some people pay 20%. If the service is poor, they pay less.

In the UK, tips of 10% are ⁵_____ in restaurants. However, tipping is not common in Australia or New Zealand.

Tipping is not required for fast food restaurants, coffee shops or ordering ⁶_____. Also, some restaurants add a service charge to the check. You do not have to tip if there is a service ⁷_____.

Finally, if you want to pay with a credit card, check that the restaurant accepts your card. In some places, when you use a ⁸_____ card, you need your PIN number. So make sure you know it!

Unit 9 — How Do I Order Food?

Checking Listen to the passage on the previous pages and check your answers.

Comprehension Think about the passage, then answer the questions below.

1. If you want to pay for a meal in the US or Canada, what do you say?
   _____

2. How much is a normal tip in restaurants in the US and Canada?
   _____

3. Is tipping common in Australia and New Zealand?
   _____

4. Is a tip required in a fast food restaurant?
   _____

5. If there is a service charge, do you need to tip?
   _____

6. In some places, do you need a PIN number when you use a credit card?
   _____

Message from Junko

When I came to the United States, I didn't know anything about tipping. I asked my host family and teachers, and they told me when to tip and how much to give.

Advice from Junko

In a restaurant, always smile and say "please." Also, you can use gestures. In the US, making a check sign (✓) with your fingers means, "I'd like the check, please!"

Useful Expressions

Phrases on the Topic Below are some useful phrases related to this unit. Check (✓) any ones that are difficult for you to understand.

In a Restaurant

1. ☐ Do you have a table for four? 　4人席の空きはありますか。
2. ☐ Can we have a menu, please? 　メニューをもらえますか。
3. ☐ What do you recommend? 　お勧めは何ですか。
4. ☐ I'm ready to order. 　注文が決まりました。
5. ☐ I'd like some spaghetti, please. 　スパゲティをお願いします。
6. ☐ I'd like to have what she is having. 　彼女と同じものをお願いします。
7. ☐ I'd like to try some local dishes. 　地元の料理を試したいです。
8. ☐ Can I have some ketchup, please? 　ケチャップをもらえますか。
9. ☐ Excuse me, my order hasn't come yet. 　すみませんが、注文したものがまだ来ていません。
10. ☐ Excuse me, I didn't order this. 　すみませんが、これは注文していません。
11. ☐ Can we have the check, please? 　勘定書をもらえますか。
12. ☐ Can I pay by credit card? 　クレジットカードで支払えますか。
13. ☐ Can we take the rest of this food home? 　残ったものを持ち帰ってもよいですか。
14. ☐ The meal was great, thanks! 　料理がとても美味しかったです。ありがとう。
15. ☐ The service was excellent. 　サービスが素晴らしかったです。

Takeout

16. ☐ I'd like to order some takeout. 　持ち帰り用の料理を注文したいです。
17. ☐ How long will it take? 　どれくらい時間がかかりますか。

Money

18. ☐ How much does this cost? 　これはいくらですか。
19. ☐ How much is 100 dollars in yen? 　100ドルは何円ですか。
20. ☐ How much is 2,500 yen in dollars? 　2,500円は何ドルですか。

Pronunciation Listen and repeat the phrases above. Say each one clearly.

Numbers | **Money**

Below is some information about the currencies used in different countries.

Countries	Currencies	Symbols		
United States	US dollar	$ = dollar, ¢ = cent	→	$1 = 100¢
Canada	Canadian dollar	$ = dollar, ¢ = cent	→	$1 = 100¢
Australia	Australian dollar	$ = dollar, c = cent	→	$1 = 100c
New Zealand	NZ dollar	$ = dollar, c = cent	→	$1 = 100c
United Kingdom	pound	£ = pound, p=pence	→	£1 = 100p
Eurozone countries	euro	€ = euro, c=cent	→	€1 = 100c

Notes

▶ In the US: a 1¢ coin is called a "penny"; a 5¢ coin is a "nickel"; a 10¢ coin is a "dime"; and a 25¢ coin is a "quarter."
▶ In Canada: there is no 1¢ coin; a 5¢ coin is a "nickel"; a 10¢ coin is a "dime"; a 25¢ coin is a "quarter"; and a $1 coin is called a "loonie."
▶ In Australia, the smallest coin is 5c.
▶ In New Zealand, the smallest coin is 10c.
▶ The euro is used in the eurozone countries, which include Austria, Belgium, Finland, France, Germany, Greece, Ireland, Italy, the Netherlands, Portugal and Spain.

Pronunciation Listen and repeat the following money phrases. Say each one clearly.

1. $1.25
2. 55¢
3. 75p
4. about £20
5. €77
6. £19.99
7. about $2,000
8. €121.50
9. $77.34
10. 99c

Unit 10

I Lost My Passport

This unit is about what to do if you lose important things such as your passport.
There is also some useful travel advice.

Warm-up ▶ Ask these questions to a partner.

1. Have you ever lost something important? If so, what happened?
2. How can you keep your passport safe during a trip overseas?
3. If you stay abroad for a month, what important things must you take with you?

Vocabulary

Keywords — Do you know the meanings of the words below? Check (✓) any ones that are difficult for you to understand.

1. ☐ calm down [v] ▶ (気持ちや態度が) 落ち着く
2. ☐ contact [v] ▶ 連絡を取る
3. ☐ embassy [n] ▶ 大使館
4. ☐ lose [v] ▶ 失くす、紛失する
5. ☐ photocopy [v] ▶ コピーする、複写する
6. ☐ possession [n] ▶ 所有物
7. ☐ steal [v] ▶ 盗む
8. ☐ tip [n] ▶ 助言、秘訣、アドバイス
9. ☐ valuable [adj] ▶ 貴重な
10. ☐ wallet [n] ▶ 財布

Pronunciation — Listen and repeat the words above. Say each one clearly.

47

Unit 10 — I Lost My Passport

Definitions

Match each word in the box to the best definition below. The first one has been done for you.

| calm down | contact | embassy | lose | photocopy |
| possession | steal | tip | ~~valuable~~ | wallet |

1. _____valuable_____ very important or expensive
2. _____ to copy a piece of paper using a machine
3. _____ to take something from another person without permission
4. _____ something that is yours
5. _____ to be unable to find something
6. _____ a national building or office of a country in another country
7. _____ a useful piece of advice
8. _____ to stop feeling excited or angry
9. _____ to communicate with someone by phone, e-mail, etc.
10. _____ a small case for carrying money and credit cards

Extra

There are some English words that have more than one meaning. For example, "tip" can mean "a useful piece of advice" or "extra money paid for a service." Here are some more examples: "check," "kid" and "race."

Dialog

Listening

Junko is in the living room, and is talking with her host father, Peter. Listen to the dialog, then answer the questions below.

1. What has Junko lost?

   _____

2. When did Junko last see it?

   _____

3. What are Peter and Junko going to do next?

   _____

87

Speaking Listen to the dialog again and read along. Then, read it aloud with a partner several times. Each time you read, change the underlined words (1–4) using the table below.

Junko: Oh, no! Peter, I have a big problem!
Peter: ¹What's the matter?
Junko: I've lost my ²passport.
Peter: Oh, Junko, that's not good. All right, first calm down. Take a deep breath.
Junko: OK.
Peter: Now, have you checked all your bags and clothes?
Junko: Yes, but I can't find it anywhere.
Peter: When did you last see it?
Junko: It was in my bag ³yesterday. I went to school, then the bank. Now it's gone.
Peter: OK, let's check your bag carefully. Then, if we can't find it, we should contact ⁴the Japanese embassy.
Junko: Thanks, Peter!

1	2	3	4
What's the problem?	credit card	on Monday	the university
What's wrong?	cellphone	the other day	the police
What happened?	wallet	this morning	your teacher

Discussion Think about the dialog above, then discuss these questions with a partner.

1. In the dialog, what do you think happened to Junko's passport?
2. Have you or your friends ever lost a valuable possession? If so, what happened?
3. If you lose something, will you stay calm or will you panic?

Unit 10 — I Lost My Passport

Passage

Pairwork — Student A and Student B have the same passage, but the gaps are different. Take turns reading the sentences aloud to your partner, and write the missing words in the gaps.

Student A

Valuable Possessions

Here are some tips about taking care of valuable possessions, such as your passport, credit card and cellphone.

Before you go ¹_____, photocopy the important pages of your passport. Take the copies with you and keep them in a safe place. If you lose your ²_____, you need the photocopies to get a new one.

When you are traveling, be careful with ³_____ items. Do not put your cellphone or wallet on a table at a cafe. Keep them in your hands or inside your ⁴_____. Also, do not leave suitcases or bags out of your sight.

While you stay abroad, keep your passport and other valuable possessions in a safe ⁵_____. One idea is to lock them inside your suitcase, then put the suitcase inside a closet.

If someone steals something from you, contact the ⁶_____ and tell your host family, a teacher or other students. If you lose your passport, contact the Japanese embassy. If you ⁷_____ a credit card, cancel the card.

Most people enjoy their stay abroad and have no major problems. You should be fine, if you follow this ⁸_____ and take care of your possessions!

89

Pairwork — Student A and Student B have the same passage, but the gaps are different. Take turns reading the sentences aloud to your partner, and write the missing words in the gaps.

Student B

Valuable Possessions

Here are some tips about taking care of valuable [1]_____, such as your passport, credit card and cellphone.

Before you go abroad, photocopy the important pages of your passport. Take the [2]_____ with you and keep them in a safe place. If you lose your passport, you need the photocopies to get a new [3]_____.

When you are traveling, be careful with valuable items. Do not put your cellphone or wallet on a [4]_____ at a cafe. Keep them in your hands or inside your bag. Also, do not leave suitcases or bags out of your sight.

While you [5]_____ abroad, keep your passport and other valuable possessions in a safe place. One idea is to lock them inside your suitcase, then put the [6]_____ inside a closet.

If someone steals something from you, contact the police and tell your host family, a teacher or other [7]_____. If you lose your passport, contact the Japanese embassy. If you lose a credit card, cancel the card.

Most people enjoy their stay abroad and have [8]_____ major problems. You should be fine, if you follow this advice and take care of your possessions!

I Lost My Passport | Unit | 10

Checking Listen to the passage on the previous pages and check your answers.

Comprehension Think about the passage, then answer the questions below.

1. What should you do before you go abroad?
   _____

2. When you are traveling, what should you not do?
   _____

3. While you stay abroad, where can you put your passport?
   _____

4. If you lose your passport, who should you contact?
   _____

5. If you lose your credit card, what should you do?
   _____

6. Do most people lose passports when they are abroad?
   _____

Message from Junko

When I lost my passport, I was really upset. But my host father helped me, and we soon found it. It was inside a book in my bag. How stupid of me! Afterwards I thanked him and we laughed about it a lot.

Advice from Junko

Take care of valuable things, especially when you are tired. If you have a problem, stay calm and ask for help!

Useful Expressions

Phrases on the Topic — Below are some useful phrases related to this unit. Check (✓) any ones that are difficult for you to understand.

Valuable Items

1. ☐ I lost my credit card. — クレジットカードを紛失しました。
2. ☐ I want to cancel my credit card. — クレジットカードを解約したいです。
3. ☐ Keep your passport in a safe place. — パスポートは安全な場所に保管しましょう。
4. ☐ Take care of valuable things. — 貴重品に気を付けましょう。
5. ☐ Do not leave bags unattended. — 鞄を放置しないようにしましょう。

Giving Help

6. ☐ What's the matter? — どうしましたか。
   ☐ — I'm worried about my friend. — 友達のことを心配しています。
7. ☐ Can I help you? — 手伝いましょうか。
8. ☐ You can borrow my dictionary. — 私の辞書を借りてもよいですよ。
9. ☐ I'll lend you a pen. — ペンを貸してあげます。
10. ☐ Don't give up! — あきらめないようにしてください。
11. ☐ Try to calm down. — できるだけ落ち着いてください。
12. ☐ Breathe deeply. — 深呼吸をしてください。

Asking for Help

13. ☐ Please help me. — 助けてください。
14. ☐ Please call the police. — 警察に電話してください。
15. ☐ Can I use your cellphone? — あなたの携帯電話を使わせてもらえますか。
16. ☐ Can you please watch my suitcase? — 私のスーツケースを見ていてもらえますか。
17. ☐ Can you please look after my bags? — 私の鞄を見張っていてもらえますか。
18. ☐ Where is the nearest police station? — 一番近い警察署はどこですか。
19. ☐ Where is the Japanese consulate? — 日本の領事館はどこですか。

Pronunciation — Listen and repeat the phrases above. Say each one clearly.

Numbers | Distance

Below are two systems for measuring distance: the metric and customary systems. Japan uses the metric system, but the US uses the customary system.

Metric System

kilometer (km) → 1 km = 1,000 m

Useful Conversion

1 km = 0.62 miles

Customary System

mile → 1 mile = 1,760 yards = 5,280 feet

Useful Conversion

1 mile = 1.6 km

🔔 Notes

▶ The spelling of some words is different in different countries. For example, the spelling is "kilometer" in the US and "kilometre" in the UK.
▶ In the UK, the customary system is called the "imperial system."
▶ These distances are also used in speeds. For example, 30 km/h is "thirty kilometers per hour" and 60 mph is "sixty miles per hour."

Pronunciation

Listen and repeat the following distances. Say each one clearly.

1. 1 km
2. 1/4 mile
3. 1/2 mile
4. 13 km
5. 3 miles
6. 30 km
7. about 25 miles
8. 875 miles
9. 1,300 km
10. about 10,000 km

Unit 11

I Need to Go to Hospital

This unit is about going to a clinic or hospital overseas. There is also some useful health advice.

Warm-up ▶ Ask these questions to a partner.

1. Have you ever been to hospital in Japan? If so, why?
2. Have you ever been bitten by an animal or stung by an insect? If so, what happened?
3. If you get sick abroad, what should you do?

Vocabulary

Keywords Do you know the meanings of the words below? Check (✓) any ones that are difficult for you to understand.

1. ☐ get stung [v] ▶ 刺される
2. ☐ have diarrhea [v+n] ▶ 下痢をする
3. ☐ medical insurance [n] ▶ 医療保険
4. ☐ medication [n] ▶ 薬、薬による治療
5. ☐ painful [adj] ▶ 痛い
6. ☐ painkiller [n] ▶ 鎮痛剤
7. ☐ pill [n] ▶ 錠剤、丸薬
8. ☐ prescription [n] ▶ 処方箋
9. ☐ swollen [adj] ▶ ふくれた、はれあがった
10. ☐ vaccination [n] ▶ ワクチン接種、予防注射

Pronunciation Listen and repeat the words above. Say each one clearly.

Unit 11 — I Need to Go to Hospital

Definitions

Match each word in the box to the best definition below. The first one has been done for you.

| get stung | have diarrhea | medical insurance | ~~medication~~ | painful |
| painkiller | pill | prescription | swollen | vaccination |

1. _____medication_____ medicine, treating illness using medicine
2. _____ a drug that stops pain
3. _____ to have an illness that makes you go to the toilet often
4. _____ a list of medicine made by a doctor for a sick person
5. _____ hurting, aching, feeling bad
6. _____ a small, round, hard piece of medicine
7. _____ become unusually large
8. _____ to feel a sharp pain when something touches your skin
9. _____ taking a drug into your body to prevent you becoming sick
10. _____ a system that takes money and pays your medical costs

Extra

A "word family" has different words with the same base. Learning word families is a good way to improve your vocabulary. Here is an example of a word family: "pain," "painful," "painkiller" and "painless."

Dialog

Listening

Junko is at the university campus, and is talking with her friend, Min. Listen to the dialog, then answer the questions below.

1. What stung Junko?

   _____

2. Where did Junko get stung?

   _____

3. What is Min going to do?

   _____

Speaking Listen to the dialog again and read along. Then, read it aloud with a partner several times. Each time you read, change the underlined words (1–4) using the table below.

Junko: Ouch!
Min: Junko, what's the matter?
Junko: I just got ¹stung by a bee.
Min: Where?
Junko: Here. It's really painful!
Min: Oh, I see, your ²neck is swollen. Try to stay calm.
Junko: OK.
Min: Do you have your student card and medical insurance card?
Junko: Yes, I think they're in my ³wallet.
Min: Can you walk OK?
Junko: Yes, I think so.
Min: Then, I'll take you to ⁴the health center. Come with me.
Junko: Thanks, Min.

1	2	3	4
bitten by a spider	leg	backpack	the hospital
stung by something	face	pocket	the clinic
bitten by a bug	arm	bag	a doctor

Discussion Think about the dialog above, then discuss these questions with a partner.

1. In the dialog, why did Min ask about Junko's student card and medical insurance card?
2. Have you or your friends ever been stung by a bee?
3. What is some good advice for staying healthy?

I Need to Go to Hospital | Unit | 11

Passage

Pairwork Student A and Student B have the same passage, but the gaps are different. Take turns reading the sentences aloud to your partner, and write the missing words in the gaps.

Student A

Health Advice

How can you stay healthy overseas? Here are some ¹_____ for keeping in good health.

Before you travel, check if any illnesses are common where you are going. Get any ²_____ and pills that are necessary.

Do you take any medication? If so, before you leave Japan, get a signed prescription from your ³_____. Buy as much medicine as you need. Also, you may want to buy medicine for common colds or ⁴_____. In some countries, such as the United States, this medicine is stronger than in Japan.

When you travel to a new ⁵_____, it is a good idea to check if the water is safe to drink. To avoid having diarrhea or other sicknesses, you can drink bottled water. Remember that ice can be ⁶_____, as well as the water you use for brushing your teeth.

Finally, try to stay healthy and fit while you stay abroad. ⁷_____ good food, exercise regularly and sleep well. This will help you to prevent illness, and also help you to ⁸_____ quickly if you get sick.

97

Pairwork Student A and Student B have the same passage, but the gaps are different. Take turns reading the sentences aloud to your partner, and write the missing words in the gaps.

Student B

Health Advice

How can you stay 1._____ overseas? Here are some tips for keeping in good health.

Before you travel, check if any 2._____ are common where you are going. Get any vaccinations and pills that are necessary.

Do you take any 3._____? If so, before you leave Japan, get a signed prescription from your doctor. Buy as much medicine as you 4._____. Also, you may want to buy medicine for common colds or headaches. In some countries, such as the United States, this medicine is 5._____ than in Japan.

When you travel to a new place, it is a good idea to check if the water is safe to drink. To avoid having 6._____ or other sicknesses, you can drink bottled water. Remember that ice can be unsafe, as well as the water you use for brushing your 7._____.

Finally, try to stay healthy and fit while you stay abroad. Eat good food, exercise regularly and sleep well. This will 8._____ you to prevent illness, and also help you to recover quickly if you get sick.

Unit 11 — I Need to Go to Hospital

Checking — Listen to the passage on the previous pages and check your answers.

Comprehension — Think about the passage, then answer the questions below.

1. What should you check before you travel?
   _____

2. If you take medication, what should you get from your doctor?
   _____

3. Is medicine for common colds or headaches the same in the US and Japan?
   _____

4. How can you avoid having diarrhea?
   _____

5. Is it always safe to eat ice?
   _____

6. How can you stay healthy and fit while you stay abroad?
   _____

Message from Junko

I was stung by a bee, but fortunately I didn't have an allergic reaction. At the health center, the nurse gave me a painkiller and some medicine. Soon, I felt fine.

Advice from Junko

Carry your ID and medical insurance card with you all the time. Also, make sure that you know the telephone numbers of your friends, your host family and the emergency services!

Useful Expressions

Phrases on the Topic — Below are some useful phrases related to this unit. Check (✓) any ones that are difficult for you to understand.

At the Clinic Reception

1. ☐ Do you have your medical insurance card? 　　医療保険証をお持ちですか。
2. ☐ Please fill in this form. 　　この書類に記入してください。

Symptoms

3. ☐ Where is the pain? 　　どこに痛みがありますか。
   ☐ — It's here. 　　ここです。

4. ☐ On a scale of 1 to 10, how much is the pain? 　　1〜10段階だと、どの程度の痛みですか。
   ☐ — It's about 2 or 3. 　　だいたい2か3です。

5. ☐ Do you have a fever? 　　熱はありますか。
   ☐ — Yes, I have a high fever. 　　はい、高い熱です。
   ☐ — I have a temperature of 38°C. 　　38度の熱があります。

Personal Information

6. ☐ How much do you weigh? 　　体重はどのくらいですか。
   ☐ — I weigh 50 kilograms. 　　50キロです。
   ☐ — I weigh 110 pounds. 　　110ポンドです。

7. ☐ How tall are you? 　　身長はどのくらいですか。
   ☐ — I'm 157 centimeters tall. 　　157センチです。
   ☐ — I'm 5 feet 2 inches. 　　5フィート2インチです。

Medication

8. ☐ How often should I take the medicine? 　　薬はどのくらいの頻度で飲めばよいですか。
   ☐ — You should take it three times a day. 　　1日に3回飲んでください。

9. ☐ Are you allergic to any medication? 　　薬のアレルギーはありますか。

10. ☐ What are the side effects? 　　副作用は何ですか。
    ☐ — You may feel drowsy. 　　眠気を感じるかもしれません。

Pronunciation — Listen and repeat the phrases above. Say each one clearly.

Numbers | Temperature

Below are two systems for measuring temperature: Celsius and Fahrenheit. Japan uses Celsius, but the US uses Fahrenheit.

Celsius (C)

Water freezes at 0°C.
Water boils at 100°C.

Fahrenheit (F)

Water freezes at 32°F.
Water boils at 212°F.

Useful Conversions

[Fahrenheit → Celsius]   □°F = (□ − 32) × 5 ÷ 9 = □°C
    For example: 80°F = (80 − 32) × 5 ÷ 9 = about 27°C

[Celsius → Fahrenheit]   □°C = □ × 9 ÷ 5 + 32 = □°F
    For example: 20°C = 20 × 9 ÷ 5 + 32 = 68°F

Notes

- °C is "degrees Celsius" and °F is "degrees Fahrenheit."
- "Celsius" is also called "Centigrade."
- −15°C is "minus fifteen degrees Celsius."

Pronunciation — Listen and repeat the following temperatures. Say each one clearly.

1. 27°C
2. 80°F
3. 13°C
4. about 30°F
5. 68°F
6. 12°C
7. about 20°C
8. 37°C
9. 98.6°F
10. −5°C

Unit 12: I Don't Want to Leave

This unit is about preparing to return to Japan. There is also information about the benefits of going abroad.

Warm-up ▶ Ask these questions to a partner.

1. If you stay abroad for one month, how will you change?
2. At the end of the time abroad, what should you do before leaving the host country?
3. Will you look forward to returning to Japan? Why or why not?

Vocabulary

Keywords Do you know the meanings of the words below? Check (✓) any ones that are difficult for you to understand.

1. ☐ active [adj] ▶ 活発な、活動的な
2. ☐ develop [v] ▶ 進歩する、成長する
3. ☐ independent [adj] ▶ 自立した
4. ☐ intercultural [adj] ▶ 異文化間の
5. ☐ major [n] ▶ 専攻分野
6. ☐ native speaker [n] ▶ 母国語話者
7. ☐ pack a suitcase [v+n] ▶ スーツケースに荷物を詰める
8. ☐ shy [adj] ▶ 恥ずかしがりの
9. ☐ solve a problem [v+n] ▶ 問題を解決する
10. ☐ tourism [n] ▶ 観光

Pronunciation ▶ Listen and repeat the words above. Say each one clearly. 57

Unit 12 — I Don't Want to Leave

Definitions — Match each word in the box to the best definition below. The first one has been done for you.

active	develop	independent	~~intercultural~~	major
native speaker	pack a suitcase	shy	solve a problem	tourism

1. _intercultural_ — involving two or more cultures
2. _____ — someone who has spoken a language since he or she was a child
3. _____ — a university student's main area of study
4. _____ — to put clothes and other things into a suitcase before traveling
5. _____ — having a lot of energy to do things
6. _____ — to find an answer for a difficult situation
7. _____ — to change and become better
8. _____ — not needing other people to help you
9. _____ — nervous to meet or talk with other people
10. _____ — traveling for enjoyment

Extra: The suffix "-ment" is a common ending for nouns. For example, "achievement," "development," "improvement" and "payment." Removing the suffix makes the verbs: "achieve," "develop," "improve" and "pay."

Dialog

Listening — Junko will soon return to Japan. She is talking with her friend, Carlos. Listen to the dialog, then answer the questions below.

🎧 58

1. When will Junko go back to Japan?
   _____

2. Has Junko changed during her stay abroad?
   _____

3. What does Junko have to do before she leaves?
   _____

Speaking

Listen to the dialog again and read along. Then, read it aloud with a partner several times. Each time you read, change the underlined words (1–4) using the table below.

Junko: I'm going back to Japan ¹tomorrow, but I don't want to leave!
Carlos: I know how you feel. Have you enjoyed being here?
Junko: Yes, Carlos, I sure have. And I think I've changed, too.
Carlos: ²In what way?
Junko: Well, when I first came here, I was shy. I didn't ask my teacher anything.
Carlos: And now?
Junko: Now, I know that it's good to speak up. My friends ask lots of questions in class and don't worry about mistakes. They're really ³assertive.
Carlos: That's good.
Junko: Yeah. I want to be like that, too.
Carlos: Great. So, do you have ⁴much to do before you leave?
Junko: I just have to finish packing my suitcase.
Carlos: Don't forget to weigh it.
Junko: I know. I don't want to pay for the excess baggage again!

1	2	3	4
the day after tomorrow	How so?	active	a lot
next Monday	What has changed?	positive	many things
in two weeks	How have you changed?	lively	anything

Discussion Think about the dialog above, then discuss these questions with a partner.

1. In the dialog, what advice did Carlos give Junko about her suitcase?
2. Do you ask questions to your teachers in class?
3. What are good things about going abroad, do you think?

Passage

Pairwork — Student A and Student B have the same passage, but the gaps are different. Take turns reading the sentences aloud to your partner, and write the missing words in the gaps.

Student A

Benefits of Going Abroad

Living abroad is a great chance for you to learn and develop in several different ways.

First, you can improve your [1]_____ ability. In class, you can learn grammar and vocabulary, and your language skills can improve. Outside of class, you have lots of [2]_____ to practice speaking and listening with your friends or host family.

Second, you might be able to learn other [3]_____ while you are abroad. For example, if your major is tourism, you may take courses in [4]_____ and hospitality. However, some students in these classes might be native speakers, so first you must study English hard!

Another area of development is [5]_____ ability. You can learn about the culture of your host country by talking with your friends and host family. Also, if you [6]_____ friends with students from different nationalities, you can learn about the culture of their countries.

Finally, you may become more [7]_____ during your stay abroad. It's normal to have some problems overseas. By solving problems, you develop personally and become more confident. Try to be flexible, and let yourself learn and [8]_____!

Pairwork — Student A and Student B have the same passage, but the gaps are different. Take turns reading the sentences aloud to your partner, and write the missing words in the gaps.

Student B

Benefits of Going Abroad

Living abroad is a great chance for you to 1._____ and develop in several different ways.

First, you can improve your English ability. In class, you can learn grammar and vocabulary, and your language 2._____ can improve. Outside of class, you have lots of opportunities to practice speaking and listening with your friends or 3._____ family.

Second, you might be able to learn other subjects while you are abroad. For example, if your 4._____ is tourism, you may take courses in tourism and hospitality. However, some students in these classes might be 5._____ speakers, so first you must study English hard!

Another area of development is intercultural ability. You can learn about the culture of your host 6._____ by talking with your friends and host family. Also, if you make friends with students from different nationalities, you can learn about the 7._____ of their countries.

Finally, you may become more independent during your stay abroad. It's normal to have some problems overseas. By solving 8._____, you develop personally and become more confident. Try to be flexible, and let yourself learn and develop!

I Don't Want to Leave — Unit 12

Checking Listen to the passage on the previous pages and check your answers.

Comprehension Think about the passage, then answer the questions below.

1. Is living abroad an opportunity for you to learn and develop?

2. Can you improve your English ability in class?

3. Can you improve your English ability outside of class?

4. How can you learn about the culture of your host country?

5. How can you learn about the culture of other countries?

6. Is it normal to have some problems when you go abroad?

Message from Junko

On the last night, I made a Japanese dish, *yakisoba*, for my host family, and gave them a present to thank them. I had a really good time in the United States, so I felt sad to leave!

Advice from Junko

You might have "re-entry shock" when you return to Japan. Here are some things to do: keep in touch with your host family and foreign friends; talk about your experiences with other students; and set an English language goal. Good luck!

Useful Expressions

Phrases on the Topic — Below are some useful phrases related to this unit. Check (✓) any ones that are difficult for you to understand.

Learning

1. ☐ What have you learned? — これまでに何を学びましたか。
   ☐ — I've learned a lot about American culture. — アメリカ文化について多くを学びました。

2. ☐ How has your English ability changed? — あなたの英語力はどのように変わりましたか。
   ☐ — My vocabulary has improved. — 語彙力が上がりました。
   ☐ — I'm better at listening now. — リスニングが良くなりました。

Self-Development

3. ☐ How have you developed? — あなたはどのように成長しましたか。
   ☐ — I've become more confident. — 以前より自信がつきました。

4. ☐ I solved many problems by myself. — 私は多くの問題を自分で解決しました。

Travel Preparation

5. ☐ Are you ready to go back to Japan? — 日本に帰る準備はできていますか。
   ☐ — Yes, but I will miss staying here! — はい、でもここでの滞在が懐かしくなるでしょう。

6. ☐ Do you have much to do? — たくさんすることがありますか。
   ☐ — I just have a few things left to do. — あと少しだけすることが残っています。
   ☐ — I have to buy some souvenirs. — お土産を買わなければなりません。
   ☐ — I need to weigh my suitcase. — スーツケースの重さを測る必要があります。
   ☐ — I must thank my host family. — ホストファミリーにお礼を言わなければなりません。

Leaving

7. ☐ Thank you for looking after me. — 私の面倒をみてくださりありがとうございました。

8. ☐ You've done so much for me. — いろいろとお世話になりました。

9. ☐ I had a wonderful time here! — 素晴らしい時間をここで過ごしました。

10. ☐ Let's keep in touch by e-mail. — メールで連絡を取り合いましょう。

11. ☐ Good bye! — さようなら。

Pronunciation — Listen and repeat the phrases above. Say each one clearly.

I Don't Want to Leave — Unit 12

Numbers | Decimals & Fractions

Below is some information about saying decimals and fractions.

Decimals

0.1 = zero point one		6.345 = six point three four five
1.79 = one point seven nine		10.108 = ten point one zero eight

Notes
- If 0 is to the right of "." you can say "zero" or "oh." For example, 1.07 is "one point zero seven" or "one point oh seven."
- Say the numbers to the right of "." as separate numbers. For example, 1.65 is "one point six five." Do not say "one point sixty-five."

Fractions

1/2 = one half	1/3 = one third	1/4 = one quarter	1/5 = one fifth
2/3 = two thirds	3/4 = three quarters	4/5 = four fifths	6/10 = six tenths

Notes
- You can also say 1/2 and 1/3 as "a half" and "a third" and so on.
- Be careful with "s" endings. If the number to the left of "/" is 1, there is no "s." For example, 1/8 is "one eighth." If the number is more than 1, there is an "s." For example, 3/8 is "three eighths."

Pronunciation Listen and repeat the following decimals and fractions. Say each one clearly.

1. 2.54 cm
2. 1.56 m
3. 42.195 km
4. 98.6°F
5. 1/2 pint
6. 2/5
7. about 1/2 km
8. 7/8
9. 9/10
10. about 3/4 mile

Review of Units 7–12

This is a review of the Keywords, Phrases on the Topic and Numbers sections in Units 7–12.

Keywords

Do you remember the Keywords from Units 7–12? Write the correct English words below.

1. 国民の祝日
2. 話題
3. いら立たしい、もどかしい
4. 快適な、楽な
5. ホームシック、郷愁
6. 成し遂げる
7. 気がふさぐ、憂鬱になる
8. 持ち帰り用の飲食物
9. 注文する
10. 勘定書
11. 財布
12. 大使館
13. 失くす、紛失する
14. 盗む
15. 医療保険
16. 痛い
17. 錠剤、丸薬
18. 活発な、活動的な
19. スーツケースに荷物を詰める
20. 自立した

Phrases on the Topic

A Do you remember the Phrases on the Topic from Units 7–12? Write the correct English phrases below.

1. 学校はどうでしたか。

2. 映画について話しましょう。

3. あなたの好きな祭りは何ですか。

4. 私は孤独です。

5. 私にアドバイスをもらえますか。

6. あなたの目標は何ですか。

7. （あなたは）ここで快適な時間を過ごしていますか。

8. （私たちに）メニューをもらえますか。

9. （私は）スパゲティをお願いします。

10. これはいくらですか。

11. 手伝いましょうか。

12. 一番近い警察署はどこですか。

13. （私は）クレジットカードを紛失しました。

14. どこに痛みがありますか。

15. （私は）38度の熱があります。

16. （あなたは）体重はどのくらいですか。

17. （私は）アメリカ文化について多くを学びました。

18. （あなたは）たくさんすることがありますか。

19. （私は）素晴らしい時間をここで過ごしました。

20. さようなら。

B The phrases below use some new words to review the Phrases on the Topic in Units 7–12. Read them aloud. Say each one clearly.

1. Let's talk about fashion.
2. What is your favorite season?
3. What do people enjoy doing here during winter?
4. I really want to eat rice.
5. I'd like to improve my listening skill.
6. I miss my family.
7. Do you have a table for two?
8. How much is 50 dollars in yen?
9. Can I have some water, please?
10. How much is 10,000 yen in dollars?
11. I lost my camera.

12. You can borrow my pen.
13. Where is the nearest hospital?
14. Do you have your student ID card?
15. I have a temperature of 39°C.
16. Are you allergic to any food?
17. My grammar has improved.
18. I'm better at speaking now.
19. I've become more independent.
20. I had a great time here!

Numbers

The phrases below review the Numbers sections in Units 7–12. Read them aloud. Say each one clearly.

1. My jacket was 5,500 yen.
2. There are about 9,000 students in my university.
3. It's 4,000 kilometres from Los Angeles to New York.
4. There are about 250,000 people in my hometown.
5. There are about 23,000,000 people in Australia.
6. The population of the US is about 320,000,000.
7. This candy costs 35¢.
8. I have about £40 in my wallet.
9. The train ticket is €78.25.
10. The cost of the food was $13.95.
11. I walked about 1/2 mile.
12. The school is about 4 miles from here.
13. I jog 5 km every morning.
14. Today's temperature is about 20°C.
15. Yesterday it was 80°F.
16. The temperature goes down to 10°F in winter.
17. It's 3/4 mile to the shop.
18. Your suitcase weighs 22.5 kg.
19. My height is 1.6 m.
20. You should put 1/2 a cup of milk in the soup.

Preparation for Departure

Checklist

Below is a list of things to do before you go abroad. Check (✓) the items that you have done.

English Communication

- [ ] I finished studying this textbook.
- [ ] I learned some useful phrases for different situations in travel/study abroad.

Information

- [ ] I know the money used at my destination, and have some cash.
- [ ] I have a credit card, and I know my PIN number.
- [ ] I made a copy of my passport, and I have a spare photo in case of losing my passport.
- [ ] I know the time difference between Japan and my destination.
- [ ] My family and friends know how to contact me overseas.

Packing

- [ ] I checked the temperature at my destination, and I have packed the right clothing.
- [ ] I packed a portable umbrella and other rain/snow gear necessary for the destination.
- [ ] I packed AC adapters for my electric appliances (eg: cellphone, PC, camera) and converters for the electric outlets suitable for my destination.
- [ ] I packed enough prescribed medication for the length of my stay overseas.
- [ ] I packed medication that I take for common colds and other general symptoms, such as headache and fever.
- [ ] I packed some photographs of Japan.

Traveling

- [ ] I checked the airline baggage rules and know the size and weight limits for my baggage.
- [ ] I weighed my suitcases and bags, and they are not overweight.
- [ ] My carry-on bag does not have any prohibited items.
- [ ] I have my wallet, passport, medical insurance card and travel tickets in my carry-on bag.
- [ ] I have chosen comfortable clothes for the airplane flight.

Homestay/Dormitory

- [ ] I know the address, phone number and email address of my homestay/dormitory.
- [ ] I have contacted my host family/dormitory and briefly introduced myself.
- [ ] I have plans for getting to my homestay/dormitory when I arrive.
- [ ] My host family/dormitory knows when and where to meet me.
- [ ] I know the members of my host family.
- [ ] I have prepared a small gift for my host family.

Questions

Answer the questions below.

1. What are your goals for your travel/study abroad?

2. What are you worried about?

3. What are you looking forward to?

クラス用音声CD有り（別売）

Communicate Abroad
──Essential English for Travel and Study
留学を成功させるコミュニケーションスキル

2016年2月20日　初版発行
2025年1月20日　第 8 刷

著　者　　Simon Cookson、田島千裕
発行者　　松村達生
発行所　　センゲージ ラーニング株式会社
　　　　　〒102-0073　東京都千代田区九段北1-11-11　第2フナトビル5階
　　　　　電話 03-3511-4392　FAX 03-3511-4391
　　　　　e-mail: eltjapan@cengage.com
　　　　　copyright©2016 センゲージ ラーニング株式会社

装　丁　　　　足立友幸(parastyle)
編集協力　　　飯尾緑子(parastyle)
イラスト　　　小川真二郎
印刷・製本　　株式会社平河工業社

ISBN 978-4-86312-277-2

もし落丁、乱丁、その他不良品がありましたら、お取り替えいたします。本書の全部、または一部を無断で複写（コピー）することは、著作権法上での例外を除き、禁じられていますのでご注意ください。